THE GERMAN ECONOMY DURING THE NINETEENTH CENTURY

Toni Pierenkemper

and

Richard Tilly

Berghahn Books

NEW YORK • OXFORD

Published in 2004 by

Berghahn Books

www.berghahnbooks.com

First paperback edition published in 2005

© 2004 Toni Pierenkemper and Richard Tilly

Library of Congress Cataloging-in-Publication Data

Pierenkemper, Toni.
    The German economy during the nineteenth century / Toni
    Pierenkemper & Richard Tilly.
        p. cm.
    Includes bibliographical references and index.
    ISBN 1-57181-063-3 (cl.: alk. paper) — ISBN 1-57181-064-1 (pbk.:
    alk. paper)
    1. Germany—Economic conditions—19th century. I. Pieren-
kemper, Toni. II. Tilly, Richard H. III. Title.

HC285 .P52 2002
330.943'07—dc21

                         2002025433

British Library Cataloguing in Publication Data

A catalogue record for this book is available from
the British Library.

Printed in the United States on acid-free paper

Learning and Information Services

College Lane, Hatfield, Hertfordshire, AL10 9AB

For renewal of Standard and One Week Loans,
please visit the website: http://www.voyager.herts.ac.uk

CONTENTS

List of Illustrations   vii
List of Tables   ix
Foreword   xii
Introduction   xiv

**Part I: The General Framework and Foundations of
   German Industrialization**

1. The German "State": Changing Boundaries   3
   Germany at the End of the Eighteenth Century, 3
   Germany during the Napoleonic Wars (1793 to 1806–15), 4
   Germany after the Congress of Vienna, 7
   Germany and the Zollverein (1834–1866), 8
   Germany and the North German Confederation (1866–1870), 9
   The German Kaiserreich, 11

2. A Quantitative Overview of Germany's Economic
   Expansion in the Nineteenth Century   13

3. Institutional and Commercial Preconditions   23
   Agrarian Reforms: The Case of Prussia, 23
   The Development of the German Zollverein, 31
   The Zollverein and Monetary Integration: The Rise
      of the Mark, 34
   The Impact of Monetary and Banking Reforms, 37
   A Methodological Note on Causality, 39

4. The Emergence of a Modern Economy   42
   Capital Formation, 42
   Labor Force, 45
     Labor in Agriculture, 46
     Labor in Industry and Handicrafts, 50
   Technology and Competition: The Case of the Iron Industry, 53

Railways and the Leading Sector Syndrome: Backward and
   Forward Linkages, 58
The Role of the State, 68

**Part II: The German Economy since the Middle of the
   Nineteenth Century**

5. Agriculture   75
   Production and Productivity, 76
   Agricultural Protection, 81

6. Population and Labor   87
   Population and Migration, 87
      Population Growth, 87
      Population Dynamics, 90
      Migration, 94
   Labor Force Development, 101
      Size and Structure, 103
      Quality of Labor, 105
      Living Conditions, 107
      Institutional Arrangements, 110

7. Money and Banking   113
   Structure of the Banking Sector, 114
   Contributions of Banks to Industrial Growth, 117

8. Entrepreneurship   123
   Social Origins and Mobility, 125
   Traditional Obstacles, 128
   Qualifications, 129
   Political Influence, 131

9. The Role of the State   135
   Mercantilist Traditions and Periodization, 136
   "New" Economic Policies, 138
      Nationalization of the Railways, 139
      Fiscal and Tariff Policy, 140
      Social Policy, 141

10. The International Economy   145
   International Trade at Mid-century, 145
   Trade Expansion, 1870–1914, 147
   Growing Protectionism after 1870, 151
   Foreign Investment, 153

Epilogue   157
Selected Bibliography   162
Index   173

ILLUSTRATIONS

MAPS

1. The Holy Roman Empire of the German Nation
   around 1750   5
2. The German Territories around 1810   6
3. The German Confederation (1815–1866)   8
4. The Zollverein (1834)   10
5. The North German Confederation (1866–1870)   10
6. The German Kaiserreich (1871–1918)   12

GRAPHS

1. Net National Product at Constant Prices (1850–1913)   14
2a. Net National Product and Industrial Production
    (1850–1913)   17
2b. Industrial Production (1800–1913)   17
3a. Production of Mining and Iron and Steel Industries
    (1820–1915)   18
3b. Production of Textile Industries (1820–1915)   19
4. Numbers Employed in Each Sector of the Economy
   (1849–1913)   20
5. Investment and Capital Coefficient (1850–1913)   22
6. The Growth of the Agricultural Labor Force in Prussia
   and Germany (1800–1913)   47
7. Rate of Return on Capital (W_R) and Rates of Growth of
   Capital Stock (W_{in}) in Prussian Railways (1841–1879)   61
8. Freight and Passenger Rates on German Railroads
   (1840–1880)   66
9. Agricultural Production   78

10. Natural Population Movement in Germany
    (1816–1980)   89
11. Principles of Demographic Transition   91
12. Demographic Indices (1867–1961)   93
13. Phases of German Transatlantic Migration (1830–1932)   96
14. Foreign Labor in Prussia (1906–1914)   99
15. Foreign Workers by Countries of Origin in Prussia
    (1906–1914)   100
16. The Development of Welfare in Germany since the
    Mid-nineteenth Century   111
17. Joint-Stock Companies Founded between 1871 and 1913   119
18. Placement of Securities in Germany (1883–1913)   119
19. German Foreign Trade in Quantity (1835–1913) and
    Value (1880–1913)   150
20. An Index of Capital Mobility (1870–1910)   153
21. Annual Yields on Domestic and Foreign Securities
    Traded in Berlin Capital Market (1870–1913)   155
22. Rates of Return on Securities Traded in Berlin and
    London Capital Markets (1871–1913)   155

TABLES

1. Life Expectancy (1816–1910)   15
2. Real Income Estimates for Ten European Countries   16
3. Composition of Investment   21
4. Principal Prussian Agrarian Reform Measures and
   Their Effects   25
5. Estimates of Agricultural Productivity Growth in
   Prussia (1800–1861)   29
6. Average Annual Net Investment in Prussia (1816–1849)   43
7. Estimated Stock of Capital and Net Investment in
   Germany in 1850   44
8. Share of Rural Population in Prussia   46
9a. Rural Social Structure in Prussia in the Eighteenth
    Century   48
9b. Rural Social Structure in Prussia and Silesia   49
10. Social Structure of Agricultural Population in
    Prussia (1861)   50
11. Labor in Industry and Handicrafts in Germany
    around 1800   51
12. Labor in Industry and Handicrafts in Germany
    around 1850   51
13. Production and Consumption per Head of Population
    in Germany compared with the United Kingdom   54
14. Additions to the Railway System in Germany
    (1835–1880)   58
15. Railway Net Investment in Relation to Investment in
    Manufacturing and in Aggregate in Germany
    (1851–1879)   62
16. Distribution of the Locomotives in Prussian Railways
    by Year of Purchase and Country of Origin in 1853   62

17. Input-Output Sectoral Relations in Germany in
    the 1850s   63
18. Coal Transportation to Berlin   67
19. Output per Hectare of Grain Crops (1800 to 1848–52)   76
20. Crop Output per Hectare (1849–55 to 1910–13)   77
21. Tariff Protection for Arable Agriculture (1883–1913)   83
22. Tariff Protection for Animal Husbandry (1883–1913)   85
23. Shares of Value Added by Major Products in Each
    Farm Category   86
24. Average Effective Protection for Various Farm-Size
    Categories   86
25. Varying Views on Population Increase from 1800 to
    1830 in Germany, Borders of 1871   88
26. Population Growth in Germany (1816–1980)   89
27. Life Expectancy and Infant Mortality in Germany
    (eighteenth to twentieth century)   92
28. German Emigration (1816–1914)   97
29. Distribution of Polish groups in the Areas of the
    Ruhr Containing the Highest Numbers of Poles   102
30. Employment Rate for the German Population
    (1882–1980)   104
31. Participation Rates   104
32. Sectoral Distribution of the Labor Force   104
33. Skill Distribution of Male Work Force (1933)   106
34. The Unemployment Rate in Germany (1887–1913)   108
35. The Growth of Real Wages in Germany (1850–1913)   109
36. The Decline in the Number of the Hours Worked in
    Germany (1860–1913)   110
37. Assets of German Financial Institutions (1860–1913)   115
38. Assets in Germany (1875–1913)   116
39a. Estimated Asset Yields and Asset Shares in Bank
    Portfolio in Germany (1880–1913)   121
39b. Assumed Asset Yields and Asset Shares in British
    Capital Market Portfolio (1882–1913)   122
40. Origins of Berlin Businessmen (father's profession)   126
41. Professional Structure in Berlin and the Distribution
    of Social Backgrounds of Berlin Businessmen   126
42. Local Origin of Berlin Businessmen   127
43. Education of Westphalian Heavy Industrialists   130
44. Fields of Study among Westphalian Heavy
    Industrialists   131
45. Political Role of Businessmen   133

46. Branches (number of businessmen) 133
47. Value of Exports Per Capita in European Areas
    (constant U.S. dollars) 147
48. Shares of World Exports of Manufactured Goods
    among European Countries (1880–1913) 147
49. Shares of Exports of Manufactures by Groups (1913) 149
50. Foreign Trade of the Great Powers in 1913 149
51. Regional Distribution of the Foreign Trade of the
    Great Powers in 1913 150
52. Foreign Investment on the Eve of World War I
    (1913–1914) 154

FOREWORD

Every book has its own history, and this one involves two sets of experience. The initial impulse came from Toni Pierenkemper while he was a Konrad Adenauer Visiting Professor at Georgetown University, Washington D.C., during the academic year 1993–94. In the course of a series of lectures and seminars on nineteenth-century German economic history, he discovered English-language literature on this subject matter to be either lacking or dated, in strong contrast to the existing literature on twentieth-century German economic history. Pierenkemper opted to put together his own set of teaching material, aided by his research assistant, Robert Daguillard, which became the first rough outline of this book. As the book began to take shape, however, Pierenkemper realized, first, that a non-native speaker faces great difficulties in writing a readable text and, second, that some of the more recent research was less accessible to him than he had thought.

Pierenkemper thus called on Richard Tilly, at one stage his academic mentor, who has been institutionally anchored in Germany for over thirty years, but was born and educated in the U.S. Tilly, who had written a short German-language book on nineteenth-century German economic history, had long entertained the idea of publishing an English-language version on roughly the same subject, but academic obligations served as a recurring hindrance to such plans. In 1998, however, his new status as emeritus professor offered him this possibility, happily in the form of a joint venture together with Pierenkemper, his former student.

This book thus combines the differing research and teaching histories of an American, on the one hand, interested in summing up some of the fruits of his thirty years of experience in Germany, and of a German, on the other hand, confronted for the first time with the radically different American system of academic study, interested in bridging the gap between the two worlds. Our hope is that this book will help American and other English-language readers better appreciate the economy of the German Federal Republic and provide insight into how and why it looks and performs as it does.

We have drawn on the help of many scholars, and are especially grateful to Ms. Brigitte Heuser, M.A., and Mr. Niko Waesche, M.A., both of the Johann Wolfgang Goethe University of Frankfurt, and Ms. Stephanie Decker, M.A., Ms. Britta Stücker, M.A., Ms. Tatjana Range, and Dr. Klemens Skibicki of the University of Cologne for their critical assistance. To them and all, many thanks.

INTRODUCTION

This book discusses the growth of the German economy in the nineteenth century. In that period, economic growth went hand in hand with the process of large-scale structural change we call industrialization, i.e., with the absolute and relative growth of industrial activity and the shifts in the employment of resources which that growth implies. Nowadays, industrialization is on the wane in advanced economies (those of Germany or the U.S., for example), where economic growth and structural change have to do with *de*-industrialization. This does not mean, however, that industrialization is a theme of purely antiquarian interest: for the same kinds of structural change that now serve as cause and consequence of economic growth—shifts in the supply of jobs for workers offer the most dramatic examples—are inextricably connected with industrialization as well. Understanding nineteenth-century industrialization, therefore, helps to understand contemporary problems of economic growth.

Other works on nineteenth-century German economic history are still available: Knut Borchardt's contribution to the *Fontana Economic History of Europe* springs to mind, as does Martin Kitchen's book *The Political Economy*, among others.[1] These economic histories, however, are now outdated. We wish to draw on a more recent body of scholarship that has focused specifically on the problems of economic growth and structural change, that is to say, on knowledge that was not yet available, or of no particular interest, to the older surveys. Second, in doing so, we wish to show that economic history—in our case, centered on nineteenth-century Germany—is not so much a set of facts about "what happened" in

1. For further references, see the selected bibliography at the end of the book.

the past that have to be discovered as a set of opinions of economic historians, a sort of collective discourse in which those historians form and test hypotheses about that past in the hope to better link it to the present. To put it differently: we are interested in a somewhat different set of facts than our predecessors were because we face a different present.[2]

Apart from the particular merits of this book, its general topic—the German economy during the nineteenth century—will be of considerable interest both to economists interested in growth and structural change and to historians interested in how economic forces interact with other aspects of national and international history. The development of the German economy in the nineteenth century is interesting as a case of "catching up" growth, facilitated by the import of new technologies from more advanced economies, such as those of Great Britain or France.[3] As we get into our topic, we shall have frequent occasion to come back to the importance of the international context of German industrialization and to the need for comparative perspectives on the latter. The nineteenth-century German economy ought to interest historians of the period as well, since it was a major determinant of the country's political development and, in particular, of its unification. The broader context of German history is therefore another point of reference to which our account will repeatedly return.

The book is divided into two main parts. The first sets the stage, so to speak, offering some general information while analyzing the foundations of German industrialization. In chapter 1 we describe the broader political framework within which the German economy has to be placed: the country's changing boundaries, the nature of the institutional links between the individual German states—in short, the road to unification. Chapter 2 offers a largely quantitative overview of the long-run growth of

2. Another way of making the same point is to say that each generation rewrites its own history—in the light of its own current problems.

3. A vast literature is devoted to the spread of industrialization since the early nineteenth century and to the question of early British leadership and its implications for "follower" countries. An early classic is D. S. Landes, *The Unbound Prometheus* (Cambridge, 1969); see also S. Pollard, *Peaceful Conquest: The Industrialization of Europe, 1760–1970* (Oxford, 1981). For a more recent statement, see N. Crafts, "British Industrialization in an International Context," *Journal of Interdisciplinary History* 19 (1989): 415–28.

the German economy from early in the century to 1913.[4] The third chapter discusses the primary institutional changes that were carried out largely during the first half of the century and which we consider to be "preconditions" for the country's industrialization. In chapter 4 we go on to describe and explain what we see as the beginnings of the emergence of a modern industrial economy.

Germany's industrial "take-off" around the middle of the nineteenth century is the point of departure for the second part of the book. From the 1850s on, Germany was well on its way to becoming an industrialized country. By the eve of World War I, Germany had become one of the world's leading industrial economies. Causes and consequences of that development are our concern. In such a short survey, we will not be able to analyze the entirety of Germany's transformation on the political, social, or even economic level. Instead, it will be necessary to concentrate on the main features and most important sectors of the economy. In this part, we look, in turn, at agriculture, population, labor conditions, banking, entrepreneurship, the role of the state, and international relations. Lastly, a brief epilogue concludes the volume.

4. For the purposes of this book, the "nineteenth century" ends in 1914, reflecting a generally accepted convention among historians that has special validity for the German case. Due to the war's outbreak in 1914, the year 1913 ends quantitative descriptions of the nineteenth century.

Part One

THE GENERAL FRAMEWORK AND FOUNDATIONS OF GERMAN INDUSTRIALIZATION

Chapter One

THE GERMAN "STATE"

Changing Boundaries

While it is possible to speak of a German economy today, it is unclear how to describe nineteenth-century Germany, which was really a mixture of several things: a geographical entity, home to an ethnic group whose mother tongue was German, a cultural entity, a nation and many states, all at the same time.

In retrospect, we know that the German drive toward unification and the creation of a nation-state lasted for almost three-quarters of the century, began well before 1850, went through several steps, including wars and revolutions, and ended only in 1871 with the creation of the Kaiserreich. These developments are best discussed following the six different constitutional stages of nineteenth-century Germany went through, beginning with the Old Empire (Altes Reich).[1]

Germany at the End of the Eighteenth Century

The Holy Roman Empire of the German Nation (Heiliges Römisches Reich Deutscher Nation) was a German State, headed by an emperor. Yet, there was no real central power, but rather a few

1. Here, one has to rely exclusively on German-language publications since the English-language literature on constitutional and political developments in Germany for the pre-nineteenth-century period is limited. See K. O. Freiherr von Aretin, *Das Reich. Friedensgarantie und europäisches Gleichgewicht, 1648–1806* (Stuttgart, 1986). Comprehensive for the entire period is H. Durchardt, *Das Zeitalter des Absolutismus*, Grundriß der Geschichte Bd. 11 (Munich, 1990).

central institutions: the juridical body known as the Reichskammergericht, or Supreme Court, which gathered at Wetzlar; the Eternal Congress (immerwährender Reichstag) in Regensburg; the Reichshofkammer at Vienna; and, of course, the person of the emperor (Kaiser) himself, who also resided in Vienna.

The Holy Roman Empire (see map 1) was basically composed of a large number of entities possessing very different degrees of power. Its territories governed themselves in many different ways and included the Habsburg Empire, the Kingdoms of Prussia and Saxony, the Grand Duchy of Baden, small principalities, as well as the more or less "free" cities such as Hamburg, Frankfurt am Main, and Lübeck, where those who were citizens chose their government. Either through wealth or kinship, powerful minorities ruled all these territories.

Curiously, certain territories belonging to heads of foreign states, such as Hanover and Schleswig (Great Britain and Denmark respectively), were also part of the Empire. Adding to the confusion, the Habsburg Empire excluded its Hungarian territories from the Holy Roman Empire and the rulers of Prussia most of their eastern territories as well.

Germany during the Napoleonic Wars (1793 to 1806–15)

Napoleon's arrival on the French and European scenes radically changed the European political landscape.[2] In 1806, Francis II, the last Holy Roman Emperor, abdicated his throne because many German states had allied themselves with Napoleon. The ensuing alliance of states became what is known as the Confederation of the Rhine, replacing the old Empire according to Napoleon's reorganization of Europe, as can be seen on map 2, which shows central Europe at the apogee of French power (1810).

The Confederation of the Rhine included certain states newly created by Napoleon, such as the Grand Duchy of Berg and the Kingdom of Westphalia with his brother Jerome as king. The restructured Kingdoms of Bavaria, Saxony and the Grand Duchy of Baden became close allies of Napoleon, while the territory on the left bank of the Rhine was directly integrated into the French

---

2. For a comprehensive survey, see E. Fehrenbach, *Vom Ancien Regime zum Wiener Kongress*, Grundriß der Geschichte Bd. 12 (Munich, 1981). Not quite as well organized is H. Durchardt, *Altes Reich und europäische Staatenwelt, 1648–1806*, Enzyklopädie Deutscher Geschichte Bd. 4 (Munich, 1990).

Map 1: The Holy Roman Empire of the German Nation around 1750 (excluding Austrian lands)

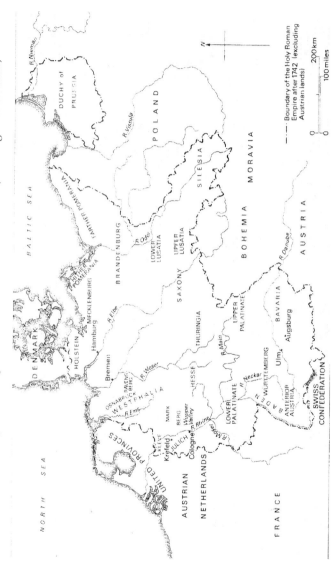

Source: M. Cerman and S. C. Ogilvie, eds., *European Proto-Industrialization* (Cambridge, 1996), 119.

Map 2: The German Territories around 1810

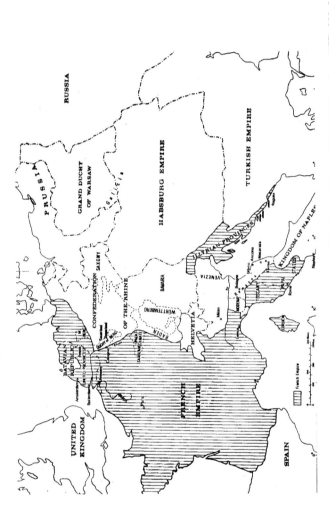

Source: A. S. Milward and S. B. Saul, *The Economic Development of Continental Europe 1780–1870* (London, 1977), 288–89.

Empire. Prussia managed to remain sovereign, but lost much of its western and central territory. The French Empire expanded deeply into northern and central Europe, annexing or subjugating the Netherlands, a large part of northern Germany including a strip stretching from Hamburg to the Baltic Sea, much of Italy including the Grand Duchy of Tuscany, the Papal States, the Piedmont, Genoa and Nice, as well as parts of the Balkans and the Illyrian provinces.

Germany as a state had almost disappeared. Before its abolition, however, the Holy Roman Empire had undertaken certain reforms, whereby the emperor and the Assembly of Members (Reichstag) accepted a new law, the Reichsdeputationshauptschluß (1803), which called for the secularization of all clerical properties by expropriation without compensation, and the integration of many small principalities in larger ones. This was in part the logical result of the peace treaty with France (according to which the territory ceded to France and located on the left bank of the Rhine was compensated for by the addition of territories from the former clerical states). In its political effects, to be sure, it went beyond mere territorial compensation. In retrospect, it became an irreversible step toward formation of a modern nation-state.[3]

Germany after the Congress of Vienna

Following Napoleon's defeat, the famous Congress of Vienna (1815) tried to partially reestablish the prerevolutionary political situation. As a result, thirty-five principalities and four free cities were created and granted full sovereignty within a new German Confederation (see map 3). The Confederation was quite heterogeneous and included the king of England (as the sovereign of Hanover), the king of Prussia, the emperor of Austria, as well as sovereigns of minor importance such as those of Saxony-Anhalt-Köthen and Waldeck, two very small principalities in central Germany.

It is nevertheless difficult to view the new confederation as a "state" in the modern sense, for there was no central government,

3. For an excellent case study, see E. Kell, *Das Fürstentum Leiningen. Umbruchserfahrungen einer Adelsherrschaft zur Zeit der Französischen Revolution* (Kaiserslautern, 1993). For the general importance of the "Reichsdeputationshauptschluß," see also H.-U. Wehler, *Deutsche Gesellschaftsgeschichte*, 3 vols. (Munich, 1987–95), vol. 1: *Vom Feudalismus des Alten Reiches bis zur defensiven Modernisierung der Reformära 1700–1815*, 363–64.

Map 3: The German Confederation (1815–1866)

Source: W. O. Henderson, *The Zollverein* (London, 1968 [1939]), before p. 1.

its borders were very loosely defined, and its inhabitants did not regard themselves as citizens of a unitary state. Its only institution was a permanent assembly of ambassadors, which gathered at Frankfurt am Main; but as events showed, it was not an effective governing organ.[4]

Germany and the Zollverein (1834–1866)

Due to the ineffectiveness of the German Confederation, the needs of the growing German economy were better served by a different institution: customs unions. The first successful negotiations toward such a union (Zollverein) produced an agreement on 19 May 1820 between Bavaria, Württemberg, Baden, the Grand Duchy of

---

4. E. Fehrenbach, *Verfassungsstaat und Nationenbildung, 1815–1871*, Enzyklopädie Deutscher Geschichte Bd. 22 (Munich, 1992).

Hessia/Darmstadt, and Nassau. This first accord—the Wiener Punktation—did not work satisfactorily, however, since only Bavaria and Württemberg really carried out the agreement. Prussia observed the negotiations between the southern states with great interest, but did not actively take part until after 1825, under the aegis of von Motz, the new finance minister. Up until then, Prussia's concern was with the economic integration of its own territories, particularly the separated eastern and western provinces (see map 3). A start had been made with the customs reform of 1818, but the western provinces remained still (geopolitically) separated from the rest of the kingdom.

Ultimately, the geographically crucial electoral state proved to be Hessia-Kassel. It was, nevertheless, Hessia-Darmstadt, not Hessia-Kassel, which cooperated in the first Zollverein (1828). For many years, Hessia-Kassel exploited its unique position and refused integration, defending its own interests founded on its own customs union, the Mitteldeutscher Handelsverein, with Hanover and, somewhat later, with Saxony.

As time went by, the commercial needs for a unitary Zollverein grew. The great breakthrough came in 1832, when Hessia-Kassel joined the Prussian Customs Union, since thereby Prussia's eastern and western provinces were directly connected to one another. Eventually, other states, such as the Kingdom of Saxony, also negotiated with Prussia, so that the Zollvereinsvertrag was signed in 1833.[5] Map 4 shows the tariff situation in Germany in 1834.

Germany and the North German Confederation (1866–1870)

The German Zollverein thus came into existence on the first of January 1834. At this time, only a few German states stood aside from the customs union, among them, Hanover with its strong ties to the English crown, Baden, Frankfurt am Main, and a few others. Most of these states, however, joined the Zollverein within a few years. And, incomplete though it was, the Zollverein served as a substitute for a nation-state during the early phase of German industrialization.

5. The history of the Zollverein is very well investigated in English-language literature. See W. O. Henderson, *The Zollverein* (London, 1968 [1939]), and also R. H. Dumke, "The Political Economy of German Economic Unification: Tariffs, Trade and Politics of the Zollverein Era" (Ph.D. diss. [unpublished], University of Wisconsin, 1976). See a recent short overview by H. W. Hahn, *Geschichte des Deutschen Zollvereins* (Göttingen, 1984).

Map 4: The Zollverein (1834)

Source: Henderson (1968 [1939]), 89.

Map 5: The North German Confederation (1866–1870)

Source: Henderson (1968 [1939]), 305.

Following the Austro-Prussian war of 1866, the German Confederation was dissolved, leaving a political vacuum. The need for a new political entity that would encompass all German states grew. A North German Confederation, heavily dominated by Prussia, was thus created (see map 5). It was more than just a new customs union, since it had its own parliament, the Zollparlament, and its own currency, the Zollvereinsthaler. The southern German states became members of the customs union, but not of the North German Confederation itself.

The German Kaiserreich

The founding of the German Kaiserreich in 1871 built on a long history of political changes, some of which have just been described. The German historical literature, particularly its older works, has interpreted the Empire's founding as the joint product of Bismarck's astute statesmanship and the striving of the German people toward national unity. Unification, to be sure, was not only an aim pursued by Germany's middle classes but also corresponded to the needs of an emerging industrial system and the great power ambitions of the Prussian State and its feudal-aristocratic elite. Fulfillment of these aims, however, depended upon excluding the Habsburg Monarchy from co-membership in a unified Germany, an intermediate goal realized through the Austro-Prussian War of 1866, and upon winning the assent of the South German states, who fulfilled this aim by joining Prussia as allies in the successful war against the France in 1870–71. On 18 January 1871, in the Hall of Mirrors in Versailles—and even before an armistice had been concluded with France—the German Empire was proclaimed, with Prussia's King Wilhelm I becoming the first German Kaiser, and Bismarck, the Prussian minister-president, the Reich's chancellor.

The newly founded Kaiserreich (see map 6), whose administration still heavily depended on members of the old Prussian civil service, existed until November 1918, the end of World War I.[6]

6. For a brief overview, see H.-U. Wehler, *Das Deutsche Kaiserreich, 1871–1918*, Deutsche Geschichte Bd. 9 (Göttingen, 1973).

Map 6: The German Kaiserreich (1871–1918)

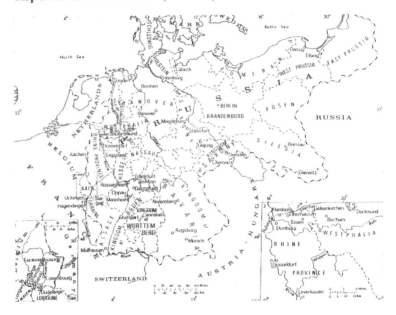

Source: Milward and Saul (1977), 18.

Chapter Two

A QUANTITATIVE OVERVIEW OF GERMANY'S ECONOMIC EXPANSION IN THE NINETEENTH CENTURY

It makes sense to begin our account of the nineteenth-century German economy with a quantitative overview. For this purpose we draw on the concept of real national product, a complex, carefully elaborated yardstick of economic performance developed mainly in the United States by the National Bureau of Economic Research (NBER) during the 1930s, especially by Simon Kuznets.[1] This is not unproblematic, for Germany had no national product statistics in the nineteenth century, and such magnitudes must therefore be estimated.

The basic technique is to take a relatively reliable estimate of real product per capita (making a useful correction for population change) for the twentieth century, in Germany's case, say, for 1913, and extrapolate it backwards through time by means of available indicators presumed to be highly correlated with real income (such as share of the labor force in agriculture, iron consumption per head, letters posted per head, etc.). Graph 1 shows the long-term upward movement of national product per head and of real wages over the period. It suggests, though the data are only rough

1. S. Kuznets, *National Income and its Composition 1919–1933*, 2 vols. (New York, 1941); C. Carson, *The History of the United States National Income and Product Accounts: the Development of an Analytical Tool, Review of Income and Wealth* (New Haven, 1975), 153–81. Note that (a) we speak of "real" national product to indicate that the measure reflects the elimination of price level changes from the series, (b) we use the term "real national product" interchangeably with "real national income," and

Graph 1: Real National Product and Real Wages (1800–1913)

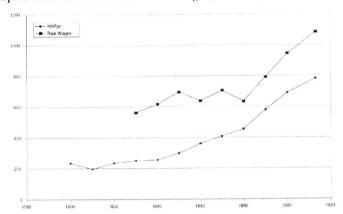

Sources: W. G. Hoffmann et al. (1965), 2d part, tables 1 and 249, R. Fremdling, "German National Accounts for the 19th and Early 20th Century," *Scandinavian Economic History Review* 43 (1995): 77–100, F.-W. Henning, *Die Industrialisierung in Deutschland 1800 bis 1914* (Paderborn, 1973), 25–28, and author's calculations; R. Gömmel, *Realeinkommen in Deutschland. Ein internationaler Vergleich (1810–1914)* (Nuremberg, 1979).

estimates, that economic growth accelerated in the second half of the century, and that the first half of the century may well have been a time of stagnation, possibly reflecting pre-industrial pauperism.[2] Note that estimated real wages, or real labor income, moved up and down over the earlier period and only entered a phase of sustained growth after about 1880.

The indicated growth of real product per capita implies an improvement in the living standards of the German population. This impression is corroborated by data on estimated life ex-

---

(c) we divide national product by population to get real national product per capita, a measure that corrects for population change. Readers may also note that in the following pages we frequently draw on the quantitative work of W. Hoffmann, *Das Wachstum der deutschen Wirtschaft seit der Mitte des 19. Jahrhunderts* (Berlin, Heidelberg, New York 1965), a historically minded economist whose work earned him the title, "the German Kuznets."

2. See T. Pierenkemper, "The Standard of Living and Employment in Germany, 1850–1980: An Overview," *Journal of European Economic History* 16 (spring 1987): 51–73. Real income per capita is closely related to the concept "standard of living."

3. For more of this kind of data see the two available handbooks on social history by (a) W. Fischer, J. Krengel, and J. Wietog, *Sozialgeschichtliches Arbeitsbuch, I (1815–1870)* (Munich, 1982); and (b) G. Hohorst, J. Kocka and G. A. Ritter, *Sozialgeschichtliches Arbeitsbuch, II (1870–1914)* (Munich, 1975).

Table 1: Life Expectancy (1816–1910) in Years from Given Age

Age	Sex	1816–60	1865–67	1901–10
0	m	26.53	32.49	44.82
	f	28.70	34.93	48.33
5	m	42.11	45.69	55.15
	f	42.99	47.46	57.27
15	m	37.97	39.45	46.71
	f	38.83	41.45	49.00
30	m	29.08	29.97	34.55
	f	29.37	30.87	36.94

Sources: W. Fischer, J. Krengel, and J. Wietog, *Sozialgeschichtliches Arbeitsbuch,* vol. 1 (Munich, 1982), 32; G. Hohorst, J. Kocka, and G. A. Ritter, *Sozialgeschicht liches Arbeitsbuch,* vol. 2 (Munich, 1975), 33.

pectancy of that population, reproduced in table 1.[3] Once again, there is a suggestion here of an acceleration in the upward movement in the second half of the century.

Germany's economic expansion was also relative. According to table 2, Germans had significantly lower incomes than the British and the Belgians, and slightly lower ones than the French up to the middle of the century. Within a generation, however, the German position had improved at least in absolute terms. One might question the precision of such estimates, and even their ordering, for example, with respect to the lead over the French economy as early as 1870. Nevertheless, the general impression of an absolute and relative improvement within the European league is plausible, and harmonizes well with other evidence of comparative industrialization patterns.[4]

Economic growth on the scale indicated implies considerable structural change, above all, industrialization. In the early nineteenth century, of course, industry represented only a small fraction of total production, with agriculture and transportation the dominant sectors. In graphs 2a and 2b we can clearly see both the initially small scale and the subsequent relative growth of the sector "handicrafts and industry"—whose share in total production rose from about 15 to well over 40 percent, 1830 to 1913.[5]

4. On this, see the locus classicus on European industrialization, Landes (1969).
5. The most comprehensive estimates of industrial production are by R. Wagenführ, "Die Industriewirtschaft. Entwicklungstendenzen der deutschen und internationalen

Table 2: Real Income Estimates for Ten European Countries (in U.S. dollars, 1970)

	1700	1760	1800	1820	1830	1840	1850	1860	1870	1880	1890	1900	1910
Great Britain	333	339	427	–	498	567	660	804	904	979	1130	1269	1302
Belgium	–	–	–	–	–	–	534	637	738	832	932	1013	1110
Denmark	–	–	–	358	382	402	489	497	563	617	708	850	1050
Germany	–	–	–	–	–	–	418	481	579	602	668	784	883
France	–	–	–	–	343	392	432	474	567	602	668	784	883
Sweden	–	–	–	–	–	–	–	292	351	419	469	597	763
Norway	–	–	–	–	–	–	–	420	441	486	548	605	706
Finland	–	–	–	–	–	–	–	300	390	407	458	529	561
Italy	–	–	–	–	–	–	–	451	467	466	466	502	548
Russia	–	–	–	–	–	–	–	236	252	253	276	342	398

Source: N. F. R. Crafts, "Gross National Product in Europe 1870–1910: Some New Estimates," *Explorations in Economic History* 20 (1983): 387–401, here 389.

Graph 2a: Net National Product and Industrial Production (1850–1913)

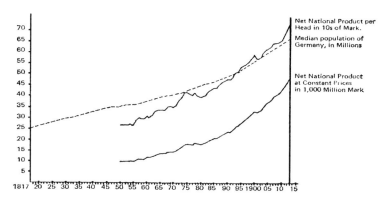

Source: Borchardt (1973), 80.

Graph 2b: Industrial Production (1800–1913)

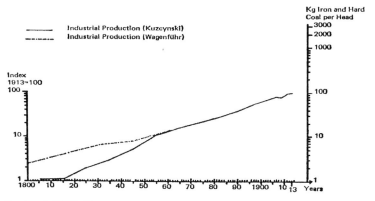

Borchardt (1973), 79.

Even within industry some remarkable structural shifts took place. Graph 3a shows the steep ascent of the output of heavy industry, but also the slowdown in the growth of coal in the last third of the century. More striking is the story of textiles, where

Industrieproduktion 1860 bis 1932," *Vierteljahrshefte zur Konjunkturforschung*, SH 31 (1933), 5–70; Hoffmann (1965).

Graph 3a: Production of Mining and Iron and Steel Industries (1820–1915)

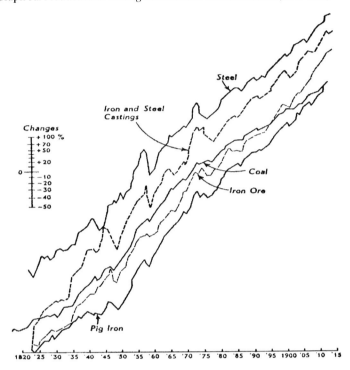

Source: W. G. Hoffmann, "The Take-Off in Germany," in *The Economics of Take-Off into Self-sustained Growth*, ed. Walt W. Rostow (London, 1969), 95–118, here 107.

cottons of course remained dynamic, while linens declined—even absolutely (graph 3b).

Structural change was reflected most clearly in the redeployment of the productive factors, labor and capital. In graph 4 one can see the predictable decline of the primary sector and domestic services, on the one hand, and the rise in importance of industrial activity and particularly of services related to communication and transport.

Roughly similar shifts in the employment of capital may be identified in available estimates of the distribution of investment. As table 3 shows, in the 1850s most investment took place in agriculture, urban housing and in railroads. Industry was a weak fourth. By the turn of the century, however, industrial investment had become dominant, though urban residential construction remained quite important.

Graph 3b: Production of Textile Industries (1820–1915)

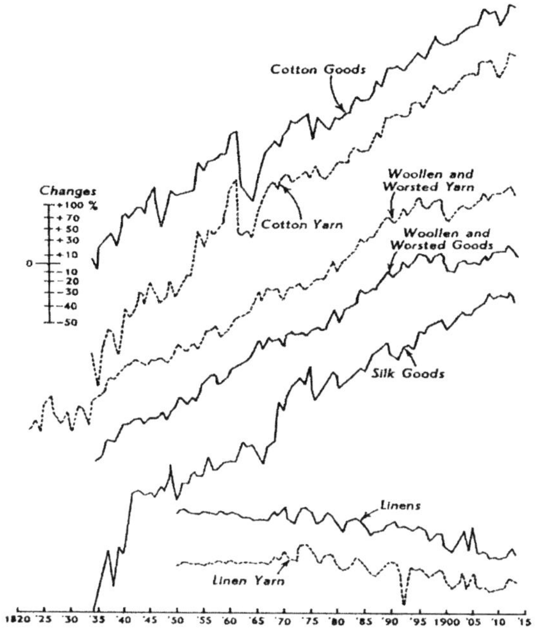

Source: Hoffmann (1969), 110.

Consideration of changes in the composition of investment lead us into a discussion of one last important quantitative aspect of Germany's long-run economic growth: its timing. This is first and foremost a question of the beginnings of Germany's modern economic growth: when did the process start? Can one divide the process into different periods? When did the initial period end? Some historians have referred to various "seminal events" and then provided varying dates for the start of the industrialization process: 1784, when the first mechanized cotton spinning mill was set up in Ratingen, near Düsseldorf (it was named after Cromford, like its English counterpart); 1789, when the first steam engine was installed in Upper Silesia (Friedrichsgrube); and 1792, when the first blast furnace began to operate with coke instead of charcoal, which also happened in Upper Silesia (though attempts to implement this process had failed much earlier in the Saar region).

These distinct events, however, were not sufficient to set in motion what one may call the process of sustained growth. Certain

Graph 4: Numbers Employed in Each Sector of the Economy (1849–1913)

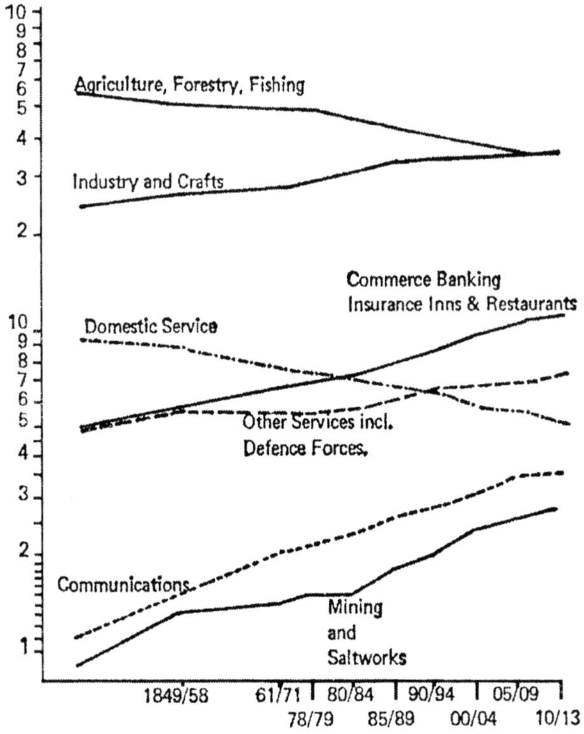

Source: Borchardt (1973), 77.

branches of industry would take decades more to develop; and more decades passed before industrial growth became decisive for the whole economy. Here, it is useful to refer to W. W. Rostow's *Stages of Economic Growth*, where the concept of the "takeoff into self-sustained growth" is developed.[6] According to Rostow, the decisive point in takeoff is reached when the overall rate of investment rises from its traditional pre-industrial level of around 5 or 6 percent of national product to over 10 percent. For Germany, there are estimates showing a rise in the rate of investment from a little

6. W. W. Rostow, *Stages of Economic Growth: A Non-Communist Manifesto* (Cambridge, 1960).

Table 3: Composition of Investment (1913 prices, in percent)

	1851–55	1856–60	1906–10
Agriculture			
Buildings	23.2	19.8	6.2
Machinery	5.1	5.6	2.1
Livestock	0.3	8.3	1.3
Inventories	6.9	9.9	0.2
Total	21.2	43.7	9.8
Industry			
Buildings	5.6	5.8	11.4
Machinery/inventories	10.5	11.3	30.2
Total	16.1	17.1	41.7
Non-agricultural dwellings	31.1	13.5	29.3
Public buildings	5.1	4.2	5.2
Underground constructions	6.4	5.0	5.3
Railways	20.2	16.7	8.8

Source: Hoffmann (1969), 115.

more than 7 percent in the early 1850s to over 10 percent in the 1860s. Graph 5 shows this increase.[7] That is one reason why we may pinpoint the beginnings of modern economic growth in Germany at around 1850, when the investment boom in heavy industry got started. Up to that point, we might argue, one can witness the establishment of the preconditions of industrial growth, but not much of that growth itself.

7. The graph also includes estimates of the capital coefficient, or ratio of capital stock to national product. The jump in investment from the 1850s to the early 1870s led the capital stock to grow more rapidly than national product. The data are from Hoffmann (1965).

Graph 5: Investment and Capital Coefficient (1850–1913): Ratio of Investment to Net National Product (in percent and 1913 prices)

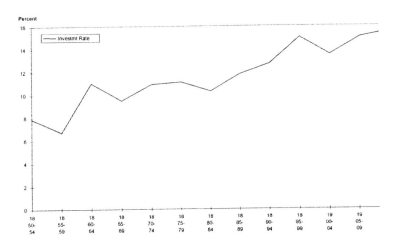

Source: Hoffmann (1969), 114.

Chapter Three

INSTITUTIONAL AND COMMERCIAL PRECONDITIONS

The industrial breakthrough of the 1850s did not emerge sponta-neously, but rather was built on important antecedents. Most German historians would accept that the period of germination in which conditions of modern economic growth were set in motion began in the late eighteenth century and stretched through the 1840s. This period included the establishment of important institutional reforms, a borrowing of industrial technologies from abroad, and other manifestations of economic modernization. In this chapter we do not discuss the role of foreign technology and focus on two, or possibly three, important "preconditions": the agrarian reforms of the century's first two decades, and the establishment of the German customs union, the Zollverein. This discussion is followed by remarks on some related and important steps toward German monetary integration and on the impact of monetary policy.

Agrarian Reforms: The Case of Prussia

After its defeat at the hands of Napoleon in 1806, the Kingdom of Prussia engaged in large-scale and wide-ranging reforms at the levels of state and society. First, Prussia reformed its army, helped by able military leaders such as Scharnhorst and Gneise-nau. It then emancipated its peasant population (*Bauernbefreiung*), granted its cities more self-governing powers (*Städteordnung*), and reformed commercial regulations (*Handels- und Gewerbegesetzge-bung*), all of which was accompanied by important changes in the system of taxation.

In German economic historiography, the emancipation of the peasantry takes center stage, mainly because the events related thereto had important implications for the formation of modern labor relations. Many contemporaries were fascinated by the *Bauernbefreiung* and a number of valuable books were published on the subject. Albrecht Judeich (1863), Georg-Friedrich Knapp (1887), von der Goltz (1893), and Max Weber (1892) all made important contributions to our understanding of the emancipation process, not so much for the accuracy of their portrayal of the emancipation process—they provide only sketchy information—as for their interpretations, which also reflected ongoing contemporary concerns with the peasant emancipation.[1]

The agrarian reforms in question had their greatest impact in the older, East Elbian Prussian territories, where near-feudal relations had hitherto predominated. They spread from Prussia to other parts of Germany, though not immediately. They were undertaken gradually and took over a half a century to complete. Three key features of the reforms deserve emphasis:

1. Emancipation of the peasants;
2. Redefinition of property rights in land; and
3. Improvements in land cultivation.

Table 4 offers a quick summary of the reforms and their chronology.

The reforms weakened the dichotomy of tenure systems that had previously characterized German agrarian society and that had marked a great divide between East Elbian Prussia and the rest of the country, namely the manorial (*Grundherrschaft*) and East Elbian estate (*Gutsherrschaft*) systems.[2] In the manorial system, peasants cultivated small farms belonging to the landlord. The

1. The great political power and high social status of East Elbian estate owners, the Junker, in late-nineteenth-century Germany ensured that the question of the reforms continued to attract interest. See Christof Dipper, *Die Bauernbefreiung in Deutschland 1780–1850* (Stuttgart, 1980).

2. A survey of the reforms can be found in the following text: K. Borchardt, "The Industrial Revolution in Germany 1700–1914," in *Fontana Economic History of Europe*, ed. C. M. Cipolla, vol. 4.1: *The Emergence of Industrial Societies* (London, 1973), 76–160, esp. 95–99. See also the much older, but still relevant, chapter in W. Bowden, M. Karpovich, and A. P. Usher, *An Economic History of Europe Since 1750* (New York, 1937), 271–81.

Table 4: Principal Prussian Agrarian Reform Measures and Their Effects

Aim of Reform	Measure	Effects
Peasant emancipation	Edict of 9 October 1807	1. Abolition of serfdom 2. Abolition of restrictions on mobility 3. Free trade in land 4. Legalized partition of entailed estates
Commutation of feudal tenures	Edict of 14 September 1811	Encouraged transformation of feudal tenures into peasant land ownership
	Edict of 29 May 1816	Restricted scope of 1811 edict
	Edict of 7 June 1821	Further restricted 1811 edict
	Edict of 2 March 1850	Widened commutation to include small peasant holdings and created land bank to finance commutation
Organization of land use	Edict of 14 September 1811	Provided for division of commons
	Edict of 7 June 1821	Procedures for division of commons and separation of holdings

peasants or tenants paid the landlord dues as compensation for land use. The tenures were customary, determined by the individual history of each land plot, and might range from a simple lease to a hereditary tenure close to legal ownership. The conditions of tenure varied correspondingly—along a spectrum that ran from strong rights and light dues to weak rights and heavy dues.

In the estate system, most characteristic of East Elbia, the landlord himself organized the tilling of the estate. He used the labor of dependent serfs and their cattle, and left them only small parcels of land on which to feed their cattle and, more importantly, their families! East Elbian estates, moreover, also had a number of state-like powers—including the obligation and right to recruit local peasants for military service in his district, to act as the local judge, carry responsibility for religious offices, pay the local priest and care for the local church. Tenants and serfs, therefore, were dependent on the landlord in all aspects of life.

Agrarian reforms implied a radical reordering of rural social and economic relationships. As such, they involved considerable risks, in particular, the risk of conflict among the affected social classes and the related risk of economic disorganization. Readiness to bear those risks was thus a prerequisite of the reforms—reforms which themselves must ultimately be seen as a prerequisite of the transition to a modern industrial society.[3]

How was this risky reform process carried out in Prussia? The first step was the edict of 9 October 1807, which led the way to a number of important changes The most important one was the grant of personal freedom to the peasantry. As table 4 suggests, this law also freed landownership from its previous dependence upon social status, provided procedures for the break-up of entailed estates and, finally, paved the way for the transformation of feudal tenures into individual property rights in land. This set of changes was clearly to the advantage of those peasants who could thereby become landowners, though they were obliged to compensate the landlords for their legal loss in the form of dues or service or their money equivalent. The reforms were implemented regionally, the first steps coming in 1808 in East Prussia and Lithuania, then in 1809 in Silesia, with Pomerania, the Ostmark, and Neumark following in 1810.

Implementation of this policy, however, involved other government measures (see table 4). Controversy arose concerning the principle of complete compensation for ownership rights. Amendments came in 1811 and again in 1816. The edict of 1811 concerned only those tenants with "weak rights" and heavy dues. "Full compensation" was abandoned and the obligatory payments were reduced to an amount based on half of the land granted. The landed gentry, in turn, believed that this edict was overly favorable to the peasantry and appealed to the government in Berlin, which found itself forced to look for a compromise solution.

The Declaration of 1816 promulgated by the Prussian government was this compromise: its net effect was to restrict the scope of the 1811 edict. As a revisionist edict, it reduced the number of peasants entitled to become landowners. Small parcel holders

---

3. A comprehensive analysis of the complex undertaking was carried out by H. Harnisch, *Kapitalistische Agrarreformen und Industrielle Revolution. Agrarhistorische Untersuchungen über das ostelbische Preußen zwischen Spätfeudalismus und bürgerlich-demokratischer Revolution von 1848/49 unter besonderer Berücksichtigung der Provinz Brandenburg* (Weimar, 1984).

and limited tenure holders were excluded from the entitlements of the reform.

This step probably made economic sense, since the recognition of small holdings would have enhanced division of the land into numerous minute parcels and might well have hurt Prussian agriculture. In addition, many of the services that serfs were traditionally obliged to render and that had been eliminated in 1811 without compensation of the landlord were restored by the Declaration of 1816.

Only in 1821 did the Prussian State undertake reforms in favor of the tenants with "strong rights" and minor dues. Up to then, the reforms had affected less than one-fifth of Prussia's cultivated land. The reason was simple: since some of the tenants had "better rights," the authorities felt it unnecessary to grant them legal ownership as well. Nonetheless, this is precisely what happened in 1821, after supporters of reform in the Prussian government had won out. Thus, a process was initiated which lasted well into the 1830s and transformed the bulk of the Prussian peasantry into landowners. To fully appreciate the impact of this reform, however, it is essential to realize that many small landholders still remained outside of the reform process. It was doubtless the Revolution of 1848–49 that led the way to a widening of the reforms. This came with the Commutation Law of 2 March 1850—so to speak a delayed result of the Revolution which ultimately gave the peasants complete legal emancipation. This same law, moreover, provided for creation of a land bank by means of which peasants could finance the purchase of their holdings. This was important since it put an end to compensation of the lords by means of peasant land. In retrospect this turned Prussia from an estate- and manorial-based rural society into one in which land could be bought and sold like any other commodity and marks its entrance into capitalism. The relationship to the emerging capitalist economy is therefore apparent.

Finally, the third aspect of the agrarian reforms deserves attention, namely, changes in the organization of land use. It is important to point out that the economic advantages of extinguishing common rights in land had long been recognized in Prussia, most recently and clearly in Prussia's "General Legal Code" (Allgemeines Landrecht) promulgated in 1794. Nevertheless, common rights remained predominant, and it was the Edict of 14 September 1811 (see table 4) that established general rules for carrying out partition of the commons. Not too much came from this measure initially, partly owing to wartime pressures (until 1815), but mainly because the rules favored defenders of the status quo and continuing common rights. In this respect the Edict of 7 June 1821 represented a marked step forward, for it not only lowered the threshold of consent of affected landholders necessary to achieve partition, but it also made separation and consolidation of individual holdings easier to execute (above all by providing clear rules for determining the value of the plots of land that were to be exchanged). A major disadvantage of the hitherto dominant "open field system" was that it tended to serve as an obstacle to innovative farmers, who could only change methods of crop rotation and other cultivation practices if all other adjacent landholders agreed to the changes.[4] Uncertainty with respect to the distribution of costs and benefits of such changes among all affected landowners would obviously dampen incentives to undertake innovation. Historians seem to agree that this aspect of the reforms positively affected incentives to invest and innovate in Prussian agriculture, but the statistical basis for the presumption is weak. A high proportion of Prussia's agricultural land holdings was affected by separation and consolidation procedures, but the amount of redistribution may have been small, for even at the end of the nineteenth century scattered holdings remained widespread. Moreover, there were "losers" of this reform, above all the landless people whose cattle had grazed on the commons.

Taken together, these three sets of agrarian reform measures amounted to a revolution in property rights, a revolution that contributed to German industrialization in several ways. First, individual property rights in land and labor presumably encouraged more efficient (or more intensive) use of those resources: peasants retained a larger share of the fruits of their labor than previously, while larger landowners, who increasingly used hired labor, were likely to employ it in a more cost-conscious manner. An important corollary of these relationships was that "surplus labor" in agriculture would be more readily recognized as such and induced to move into non-agricultural employment. The "payoff" was, at least in the long run, increased productivity in agriculture. Of

---

4. Under the traditional "open field system," individual peasants typically held usage rights to scattered plots of land, the scattering being a way of ensuring a more or less equitable distribution of good and bad land among landholders, perhaps also a means for providing a degree of diversification. This created, then, a spatial distribution of land by crops and function rather than by ownership, with many owners sharing the same fields for each crop and function.

Table 5: Estimates of Agricultural Productivity Growth in Prussia (1800–1861) (annual rates of growth in percent)

Period	Value Added per Worker[a]	Period	Gross Output per Worker, Prussia (in tons)[b]	Gross Output per Worker, East Elbian Prussia (in tons per ha.)[b]1
1816–1822	1.61	1800–1840	0.44	1.29
1822–1831	2.59			
1831–1840	1.46	1840–1860	0.79	2.13
1840–1849	1.09			

[1]Agricultural land in hectares.

Sources: (a) R. Tilly, "Capital Formation in Germany," in *Cambridge Economic History of Europe*, vol. 7 (1978), 382–441; (b) R. A. Dickler, "Organization and Change in Productivity in Eastern Prussia," in *European Peasants and Their Markets*, ed. W. N. Parker and E. Jones (Princeton, 1975), 286.

course, there are problems in estimating such effects. For one thing, reforms had their greatest institutional impact in East Elbia, where agricultural productivity remained significantly lower than in the less reform-oriented West. In addition, the overall data on agricultural outputs and inputs for the first half of the century are poor. Nevertheless, a substantial increase in land and labor productivity in Prussia over the period seems most probable. Table 5 provides two measures of these, one for Prussia as a whole and one for East Elbian Prussia. The first is based on a value-added measure of (net) output, the second on a measure of (gross) physical output, both expressed as rates of growth per year. The latter is an estimate of total crop production expressed in tons (column 2). Without reforms, one may hypothesize that productivity increases such as these would have been much less likely.

The reforms also had significant effects on wealth distribution and social structure. The Prussian (and later German) reforms forced the peasantry to pay for emancipation and for their land. Assuming that pre-reform land use reflected true ownership claims—not the assumption of Prussian reformers—one could interpret the reforms as a vast redistribution of resources in favor of the aristocratic estate owners. Considerable sums changed hands between circa 1821 and 1850 (the period in which about 90 percent of the relevant land claims were settled), they amounted (according to one estimate) to cash payments of 243 million marks and land transfers worth about 84 million marks, which adds up to

327 million marks, or 10 million per year. That is more than the esti-mated annual net investment in Prussia's industrial sectors in this period. Two consequences flowed from this transfer. One was the further impoverishment and marginalization of smallholders and the landless whose existence had in part depended upon access to the now "privatized" commons. This social stratum became the basis of a rural proletariat, as Georg Friedrich Knapp argued so long ago, and it also filled the ranks of migrants on their way abroad or into non-agricultural employment elsewhere in Germany.[5] A sec-ond consequence was the social and economic strengthening of the aristocratic landed estate owners in Prussia, although the putative effects on economic growth are ambivalent. On the one hand, inso-far as these estate owners were less efficient than peasant farmers, the transfer could be said to have held back economic develop-ment compared to what a conceivable alternative institutional arrangement might have produced. On the other hand, as benefi-ciaries of the new system of property rights, those landlords be-came, at least tacitly, one of its most important supporters. This made them more likely allies of the ascendant urban bourgeoisie, and probably enhanced the country's social and political stabil-ity—a positive input into the industrialization process.

Before leaving this topic, we wish to stress yet a third effect of the reforms in Prussia, one which has not always received the credit due, but which recent scholarship, above all that of Hartmut Harnisch has well documented: we mean the survival of the mid-dle peasantry as a socio-economic class, a fact which was to have considerable political importance, as we shall see later, but which was also partly responsible for the increased productivity in agri-culture already mentioned.[6] The survival of the peasantry as social class and economic actor, it is worth noting, meant that German industrialization represented, at least until the end of the nine-teenth century, a sharp contrast to that of Great Britain.

---

5. G. F. Knapp was the author of a landmark study, *Die Bauernbefreiung und der Ursprung der Landarbeiter in den älteren Teilen Preussens*, 2 vols. (Munich and Leipzig, 1927 [1887]).

6. As Harnisch has more recently pointed out, Knapp's deservedly much-cited study concentrated single-mindedly on the negative effects of marginalization of the landless, and neglected the gains of the middle and upper peasantry. See Har-nisch, "Georg Friedrich Knapp, Agrargeschichtliche Forschung und sozialpolitis-ches Engagement im Deutschen Kaiserreich," *Jahrbuch für Wirtschaftsgeschichte* 1 (1993): 95–132, esp. 118–19.

The Development of the German Zollverein

Commercial policy represents a second important area of institutional change which took place during the first half of the century and which powerfully shaped subsequent development. At the heart of this story is the Zollverein, seen by so many as the basis and initiator of German industrialization and of German unification. In the historiography we find the legend of the Zollverein as a successful means of overcoming British commercial supremacy and in paving the way for the Wilhelminian Empire. The great Prussian historian, Heinrich von Treitschke, rated the Zollverein as the "glorious beginning of a glorious history." In his view, the Zollverein represented a triumph of the Prussian state and "Prussian Way" toward modernity, the achievement of magnificent statesmen and civil servants. A more realistic interpretation did not appear until 1939 with William O. Henderson's *The Zollverein*, which called Treitschke's conclusions into question.[7] Since then, many further modifications on the original story have been made, up to and including analogies drawn between the Zollverein and post-1945 efforts toward European integration.[8] The key question remains, however, the extent of the Zollverein's contribution to creation of a unified German market.

Understanding the role of the Zollverein entails in any case an examination of its beginnings. As in the previous section, we may usefully begin with the Napoleonic period. Napoleon's "Continental System" allowed a relatively free exchange of goods inside the Napoleonic territories, but maintained relatively high tariff barriers on foreign products and even an economic blockade against Britain. Napoleon's defeat meant the demise of this continental system of tariffs. In its place, partly as a result of the Congress of Vienna in 1815, new barriers emerged, specific consequences of which are worth mentioning. First, the "infant industries" established under the Continental System were now subjected to international competition, and above all, to that of Great Britain, well into its "industrial revolution," and suffered

---

7. W. O. Henderson, *The Zollverein* (Cambridge, 1939); H. von Treitschke, *Deutsche Geschichte im 19. Jahrhundert* (Leipzig, 1908).

8. On this, see W. Fischer, "The German Zollverein: A Case Study in Customs Union," *Kyklos* 13 (1960): 65–89; also the more recent collection by H. Berding, ed., *Wirtschaftliche und politische Integration in Europa im 19. und 20. Jahrhundert* (Göttingen, 1984).

severe setbacks.[9] Due to their superiority in quality and price, British producers returned to central European markets with a vengeance, and became dominant. Second, a number of European powers introduced new tariff barriers. In 1816, for example, France's new protective tariffs effectively sealed off its markets from foreign producers, and Germans were particularly hard hit. The British corn laws, introduced in 1815, protected British agricultural producers against Prussian exporters; and the union of Holland with the Southern Netherlands (later Belgium) was an additional blow to German fledgling industries.

The next step in the story concerns the Prussian Customs Union of 1818. Partly a response to the changes in European commercial policy just mentioned, it was also designed to foster the administrative and political as well as economic integration of Prussia's new western and central territories with its older, eastern base.[10] This had four effects. First, it was a fiscal success. The new system generated larger net revenue gains than had been anticipated—gains which resulted from a substantial savings in collection costs and which were all the more welcome as they were free of the political restraints that burdened changes in direct taxes (e.g., negotiations with those quasi-parliamentary bodies, the Stände, or Estates Assembly). Second, it reduced internal tariffs and, by providing modest protection against foreign producers, facilitated internal trade and hence the economic integration of Prussia, particularly between the East and the industrially more advanced West. Third, the law of 1818 can be viewed as a triumph of the liberal, free trade principles esteemed by Prussia's civil servants, for the tariffs were relatively low, offering but modest protection for manufactured goods (effectively about 10 percent), designed to permit duty-free import of raw materials and basically conceived as a revenue machine. Fourth, and finally, the Union of 1818 led to shifts in the geographic pattern of trade and affected other German states whose trade crossed Prussian borders. The efficiency and impressive fiscal results put pressure on neighboring states to follow the Prussian example.

9. The locus classicus on the Continental Blockade and the British economy is F. Crouzet, "Wars, Blockade, and Economic Change in Europe, 1792–1815," *Journal of Economic History* 24 (1964): 567–88.

10. The reader is reminded that Prussia's foothold in the west was greatly expanded as a result of the Napoleonic War settlement that the Vienna Congress brought about. An excellent study of the customs union of 1818 is by T. Ohnishi, "Zolltarifpolitik Preußens bis zur Gründung des deutschen Zollvereins. Ein Beitrag zur Finanz- und Außenpolitik Preußens" (Ph.D. diss., University of Göttingen, 1973).

One example can illustrate how the Prussia's Union of 1818 could be expanded. The first states to join the Union were foreign enclaves within Prussia, such as Schwarzburg-Sonderhausen, which, in 1819, was the first to conclude a customs treaty with Prussia. The enclaves had previously created a problem for Prussia because of smuggling: they imported foreign goods duty free and sold these to Prussian customers inside the enclave or outside it without paying duties because of the absence or insufficiency of border controls. Tightening border controls was not a real financial solution to the problem since monitoring the borders of these enclaves proved to be extremely expensive in comparison to the gain from levying duties. The concluded treaty set a precedent: in exchange for relinquishing control over foreign trade to Prussia, the enclave state obtained a generous financial bargain. Other enclaves followed the example of Schwarzburg-Sondershausen, such as Schwarzburg-Rudolstadt (1822), parts of Saxony-Weimar (1823), Saxony-Coburg-Gotha (1824), Hessia-Homburg (1829) and Oldenburg (1830).

Not all foreign enclaves were so easily integrated into Prussia's system, and other bordering states, not to mention the non-contiguous South German states, proved much more reluctant to sacrifice their autonomy for expected financial gains. In fact, one of the features of the critical 1820s was the series of efforts to form alternative customs unions. By 1828, indeed, three customs unions existed in Germany. Nevertheless, Prussia persisted. In 1828 it had obtained the accession of Hesse-Darmstadt, a border state in financial need, to its union; but in 1831, partly as a result of fears of the ruling elite which had been stimulated by the revolutions of 1830, Hesse-Cassel agreed to join, giving Prussia its coveted direct link between East and West. In 1833 the Bavarian-Württemberg Union also agreed to join. Thus was born, to go into effect on 1 January 1834, the larger system that became known as the Zollverein. Since it consisted of a system of treaties of limited duration between sovereign states, the Zollverein's founding by no means guaranteed its continuance. Nevertheless, the 1830s represented a period of commercial expansion which yielded substantial increases in customs revenues to the member states (of about 5 percent per year per capita between 1834 and 1842). This, more than anything else, made renewal in the 1840's most likely, if not inevitable.[11]

---

11. See the penetrating analysis by R. Dumke, "Der deutsche Zollverein als Modell ökonomischer Integration," in *Wirtschaft und politische Integration*, ed. H. Berding

These institutional changes, we would argue, greatly increased the probability that a German-wide national market for goods and services would develop. It seems likely that the Zollverein's "trade-creating" effects outweighed its "trade-diverting" influence; and there is evidence that protection of "infant industries" had benign effects.[12] Two further results also deserve mention. One concerns railroad building. The Prussian and German-wide customs union influenced the regional flow of trade and called the attention of affected states—and, indeed, of local interests in the most important cities—to the importance of transport improvements to ensure one's own share of trade. The establishment of the Zollverein made the competition for trade more likely to result in increased transportation facilities than would otherwise have been the case. Railroad building since the 1840s assumed the role that road building had played in the 1820s (a point to which we will return in the next chapter). A second lasting contribution of the Zollverein to German industrialization was the impetus it gave to monetary integration. This "effect" is of such fundamental importance that it deserves somewhat more detailed treatment below.

The Zollverein and Monetary Integration: The Rise of the Mark

In contrast to post-1945 European integration, the German "common market" pushed monetary integration from the very beginning. This followed from the Zollverein's great fiscal importance, discussed above, but also from the nature of the monetary problem of the times. In the 1820s, something like 80 percent of the monetary circulation in the German states consisted of metallic coins. Even wholesale trade, which dominated interregional trade among the German states, made considerable use of silver and gold coins. The main problem stemmed from the widespread minting by German states of low-weight coins whose nominal value exceeded their value in silver. These states, that

---

(Göttingen, 1984), 71–101; H.-W. Hahn, "Hegemonie und Integration. Voraussetzungen und Folgen der preußischen Führungsrolle im Deutschen Zollverein," in *Wirtschaft und politische Integration*, ed. H. Berding (Göttingen, 1984), 45–70.

12. On trade-creating versus trade-diverting effects, see Dumke (1976); on the protective effects, see R. Fremdling, *Technologischer Wandel und Internationaler Handel im 18. und 19. Jahrhundert* (Berlin, 1986), esp. 117–37 and 205–307.

is, exacted seignorage charges on the coins they produced, but that potential source of loss to private traders was exacerbated by the fact that such charges varied across the German states and from coin to coin. In order to reduce the risk of losses through exchange of money, traders had to either spend time inspecting the coins or pay a money dealer (or banker) to do so for them. This obviously raised the transaction costs of intra-German trade.

The basic difficulty, just described, was compounded by the existence in Germany of several different monies of account, of which the two most important were the taler, which circulated in Prussia and many North German states, and the South German gulden, both based on silver. This meant that traders who had to make use of these coins had to first ascertain the gulden or taler value of coins belonging to each system, and then to negotiate the appropriate gulden-taler exchange rate.

The German Zollverein put pressure on the member states to standardize currencies, for apportionment of customs revenues among those states called for agreement on exchange rates between the different monies. Since revenues were the Zollverein's chief raison d'être, this was a serious matter. Two coinage treaties in the 1830s were the quick response. In 1837 the Munich Coinage Treaty bound the most important states of southern Germany to the following: the silver value of gulden coins was to be at least 90 percent of the respective nominal values (i.e., seignorage charges were to be limited to no more than 10 percent); the gulden was to become the legal tender in all signatory states; but the states remained free to circulate as much small-denomination coins as they wished. One year later in the Dresden Coinage Convention, the Munich Treaty was extended to cover all Zollverein states and in particular to link the taler system with its gulden counterpart. The two currencies were to be linked to silver at a fixed rate, expressed in "Cologne fine marks" and equivalent to 233.855 grams of fine silver. This unit was equal to 14 taler and 24.5 gulden. Thus, one taler would equal 1.75 gulden (while a gulden, it follows, would equal four-sevenths of a taler). In addition, the states were obligated to convert—on demand and at no cost to the holders—their small coin presented in lots of 100 taler or more into the heavier gold and silver coins. Finally, a common silver coin worth 2 taler (and 3.5 gulden) was to be introduced, which was to have legal tender status in all member states. It earned the nickname "Champagnertaler," since its value matched the price of a bottle of champagne.[13] The minting of a Zollverein coin was nevertheless an important precedent.

The next important step toward Germany's monetary integration came with the Vienna Coinage Treaty of 1857. The treaty reflected Austria's strong interest in joining the Zollverein, but even apart from that issue—since Austria never did become a Zollverein member—it was important, for it achieved three things. First, it further strengthened the status of the taler in relation to the gulden. It did this by setting the parities between taler, gulden, and Austrian florin at 1 taler = 1.5 Austrian florin = 1.75 gulden, which meant that Austria oriented its currency toward the taler, rather than the gulden. In addition, legal tender status within the member states was extended to the one-taler coin; and since this time, most of the increase in the Zollverein's coin circulation derived from the minting of the one-taler coins.[14] Second, the treaty once again confirmed the primacy of the silver standard as the basis of the union's currency, thus rejecting Austria's suggestion to move to the gold standard. And third, for the first time in this period a treaty among German states explicitly dealt with the issue of paper money, in this case including an article that banned the use of non-convertible paper money and which was, in effect, directed against Austria, a country with a traditionally large circulation of non-convertible government paper money. This was important, for quite a number of other German states had paper money in circulation. The treaty thus underscored the members' intent to maintain the convertibility of that paper into "hard money" and, hence, their strong commitment to monetary stability.

The final and best-known step toward Germany's monetary integration came of course with the country's political unification in 1871. There was an important, though often forgotten, intermediate step which is worth mentioning, however. It followed from Prussia's defeat of Austria in the war of 1866. That eliminated

13. This was too high a denomination to be of much use in the retail markets of the time, and its circulation did not grow much in the following decades. See C.-L. Holtfrerich, "The Monetary Unification Process in Nineteenth-Century Germany: Relevance and Lessons for Europe Today," in *A European Central Bank? Perspectives on Monetary Unification after Ten Years of the EMS*, ed. M. de Cecco and A. Giovannini (Cambridge, 1989), 216–41.

14. Moreover, debts contracted in either taler or gulden could henceforth be repaid in taler coins, but the reverse was not allowed. This meant that the triumph of the taler in Germany, as C. Holtfrerich has argued (1989, 224), was now complete.

Austria from the German coinage union, of course. More importantly, however, the North German Confederation which resulted
in 1867 from that war called for the shift of monetary sovereignty
from member states to the Confederation. In 1870 the same principle was applied to bank notes and government paper money
(hitherto treated as "money substitutes," but not "money"). With
the foundation of the Empire in 1871, the same rules were accepted by the states of southern Germany. Control over these
forms of money was to reside in the central government. The
reforms which then followed are well known. A new currency
came into being: the mark, divided into 100 Pfennigs and equal to
one-third of a taler; the gold standard was established in place of
the old silver standard, the transition (which, after all, was costly)
was easily financed with the five billion gold francs in reparations
obtained from France as a result of its defeat in the war of 1870;
and with the founding of a new, central bank, the Reichsbank,
which began operations in 1876, centralization of bank note issue
was insured and a unified, standardized German currency came
into circulation for the first time.

The Impact of Monetary and Banking Reforms

The monetary integration that closely followed the Zollverein
was also part of a broader set of changes in the organization of
Germany's monetary and banking system in this period. If we
were to widen our account to include these changes and the
period of the 1850s and 1860s, we would need to consider the
emergence of a strong central bank of issue, e.g., the Bank of Prussia, in addition also the appearance of new, joint-stock banks,
and, finally, a related, substantial increase in the supply of money
based on bank credit and bank deposits (most of the growth of
nearly 5 percent per annum, 1850–70, was attributable to increased bank deposits). So great were the changes in the 1850s
that at least one author (D. Landes [1956]) once described them as
a "financial revolution." Be that as it may, there can be no doubt
that Germany's monetary and banking system underwent a very
significant transformation in these years. Since economic growth,
at least in retrospect, seems to have significantly accelerated at
about the same time (and especially in the 1850s), the question of
the impact of monetary changes on economic growth does present itself. Space limitations of this volume preclude a thorough

treatment of the question; but it is of sufficient general importance to deserve at least a brief commentary.

The historiography of this issue, we stress, is ambivalent. It is
ambivalent on both the question of the relative contributions of
public and private agents and on the relevant growth mechanism.
The role of the state and of government policy was no doubt
important; but what was its effect? On the one hand, the Prussian
government—and the governments of many other German states
as well—undertook reforms of the coinage, established banks of
issue, and pursued cautious financial policies which demonstrated,
taken as a whole, a strong commitment to monetary stability.
Such a policy stance—which was accompanied by falling rates of
interest from the 1820s to the 1840s—could be said to have encouraged capitalists to invest more in real assets and, hence, in the
promotion of economic growth, than they would have done in the
presence of a laxer set of government financial and monetary policies. In modern terminology, one might speak here of a "crowding
in" of private investment caused by a parsimonious policy of
public finance. Here, one notes, the emphasis is on the positive
response of private capital supply to the state-induced financial
stability. On the other hand, the policy of parsimony described
also included a restrictive stance vis-à-vis private economic agents,
e.g., the withholding of concessions for joint-stock banks, especially banks of issue. Insofar as important elements of the economy's infra-structure, e.g., transportation and communication
facilities, depended on public spending, and insofar as such spending and a more liberal policy toward private financial institutions
might have encouraged more spending in the aggregate, given
the presence of substantial underemployed resources in the German economy of the period, one might say that the realized rate
of growth of real output per capita would have been lower than
the potential. Here, emphasis is on the negative effects of restrictive state policies, as well as on the potential positive effects of
more spending. It represents a different view of how monetary
reforms affect economic growth.[15]

---

15. With some exaggeration, we might speak of a "Keynesian" situation in which
demand, rather than supply, is the bottleneck. Its appropriateness depends on how
one should interpret the evidence on underemployment of the period from the
1830s to the 1850s. For one attempt, see R. Tilly, *Vom Zollverein zum Industriestaat. Die
wirtschaftlich-soziale Entwicklung Deutschlands 1934 bis 1948* (Munich, 1990).

There is yet another perspective, however, that enhances the degree of ambivalence surrounding the issue. An important part of the transformation of the monetary and banking system derived from the efforts of thousands of individual private agents—bankers, merchants, security traders, industrial entrepreneurs, etc.—who proved ingenious in the development of new and more efficient ways of implementing financial transactions, e.g., the use of "dry" bills of exchange (bills drawn by businessmen against their own bank accounts) as means of payment where and when the supply of paper money or bank notes seemed to be lagging behind the demand. In this perspective a restrictive government policy stance need not have held back economic growth if private agents were able to devise satisfactory substitutes for the financial institutions and instruments the government denied. Thus, the question of impact on growth posed above really requires a two-stage answer: one that identifies the presence of a shortage or surfeit of supply of finance relative to demand; and one that considers the locus—whether public or private—of undersupply and oversupply. These are basically empirical questions. On present evidence, there is much to be said for a "two-stage" view: in the period immediately following the Napoleonic Wars, monetary and financial reforms contributed to an overall stability which was conducive to capital accumulation by private agents and to economic growth; but over time, say, by the late 1830s, the restrictive public policy stance, by hindering the growth of new financial institutions, probably held back economic growth. These are no more than speculations, to be sure; but they possess sufficient plausibility to deserve further attention.

A Methodological Note on Causality

The topic of monetary integration is well suited to illustrate an important methodological point. At the chapter's outset we insisted that Germany's economic expansion depended upon the establishment of certain preconditions, above all, on institutional changes that set the stage, so to speak, for the investment and reallocation activity that carried growth forward. The naive view envisions a two-stage process:

(1) fulfillment of a precondition → (2) economic growth

Critical readers will recognize, however, that a reverse chain of causation is conceivable:

(1) economic growth $\rightarrow$ (2) establishment of preconditions

Strictly speaking, therefore, some thoughts on the identification of the direction of causation are needed. Somewhat less naive is the related idea of the "counterfactual." By this we mean the hypothesis that had the preconditions remained missing, or less fully established in the period observed than actually was the case, then economic growth would have been slower, or would have come later than historically observed.

None of the three preconditions discussed in this chapter were wholly fulfilled before German industrialization accelerated. The ambivalence of the connection is particularly clear in the case of monetary integration, for the unified monetary system that emerged in the 1870s came at the end of nearly forty years of negotiations and partial agreements: it was not the case that we see, first, monetary integration, and then economic growth. Both kinds of change took place at the same time and were mutually self-reinforcing in their positive effects. Economic growth went hand in hand with expanding interregional trade and demands for more efficient means of effecting interregional payments. Even more important is the question of counterfactuals. Metal coins, the basis of the monetary system in the early decades of the century, became less and less important for interregional trade as time went by, since traders were willing and able to substitute bank notes or bills of exchange drawn on their bankers for the metallic monies they might have otherwise used. Indeed, the use of such "credit money" would have been cheaper for large transactions than coins. The importance of integration of the coinage system, therefore, cannot hinge on the use of money as a means of payment.

What about the use of money as a unit of account? Surely, a less integrated German system of coinage would have enhanced uncertainty concerning interregional transactions on current and capital account. This is a stronger argument. Nevertheless, it is worth thinking a bit about the alternative: interregional transactions would have come to resemble international ones, in which the currency of account was linked to one of the precious metals, gold or silver, and the exchange rates tended to fluctuate around the gold and silver import and export points. If fluctuation of exchange rates are then taken as an index of how risky international transactions were in relation to interregional ones, then we could hypothesize that the ratio of international to intra-German exchange rate fluctuations could be used as a measure of how much integration contributed to internal stability (and, presumably, to readiness to invest or trade). Crude comparison suggests that internal integration did have a payoff, but the quantitative evidence is not overwhelming. The point can be generalized: the case for the relevance of preconditions remains strong, but it is more in the nature of a plausible hypothesis than an established truth.

Chapter Four

THE EMERGENCE OF A MODERN ECONOMY

The development of "preconditions" of industrialization described in the previous chapter permitted the German economy to better exploit its productive resources, i.e., its "growth potential." Growth potential depended, in turn, on the supply of capital and labor and on the interaction of technical progress and competition. These form, then, the subject of this chapter—which at the same time offers an explanation of how modern industrial growth came to dominate the German economy (in the third quarter of the nineteenth century). For the sake of convenience, our explanation moves at some points back to the very beginning of the century, at others beyond its third quarter. Nevertheless, the chapter's central theme is the emergence of a modern economy and of industry, rather than its maturity—a theme, as we will see, which really belongs to the early twentieth century.

Capital Formation

Our discussion begins with an examination of the phenomenon of capital formation. By this we mean the creation of physical means of production which took the form of plant and equipment (machines, tools, transportation facilities, etc.). We also recognize the importance of "human capital" and "financial capital," but for the purposes of this chapter the notion of capital as an accumulation of physical means of production is more suitable, not least of all because the historical literature has focused almost exclusively upon it. In a sense, industrialization can be viewed as a process in which productive methods became more and more capital intensive. One astute observer of nineteenth-century industrialization, Karl Marx, for example, entitled his now famous work *Das Kapital* in order to stress the importance of capital in the production process. He called the first volume *The Production Process of Capital,* the second *The Circulation Process of Capital,* and the third *The Total Process of Capital* (which was completed by Engels). For many years economists and economic historians tended to follow Marx in his emphasis on the role of capital. Since the 1960s, however, this view has come under challenge. The challenge also applies to Germany's industrialization. Thus, by looking closely at the available quantitative data, we find that industrial capital accounted for only a modest share of net investment before 1850.[1] Moreover, industrial growth appears to have accelerated well before industrial investment did, the 1840s being the key example. For Prussia, Germany's largest economy, see the estimates in table 6.

Notice that by far the greatest change took place in non-agricultural construction and in transportation facilities. One could see this as evidence of infrastructure investment that helped pave the way for the surges of industrial investment that were to follow (this is discussed in the section on Technology and Competition). As of 1850, however, industry's share was low. At that time, the

Table 6: Average Annual Net Investment in Prussia (1816–1849)
(millions of marks, 1913 prices)

Year	Agriculture	Non-agric. Buildings	Transport	Industry	Total
1816–22	86.5	28.7	7.0	2.8*	125.0
1822–31	70.4	18.7	8.8	5.1*	103.0
1830/31–40	109.6	52.0	22.5	5.6	189.7
1840–49	59.9	69.2	73.7**	7.0	209.8

*"Guesstimate" based on extrapolation of capital-product value trend, 1830–49 to 1816, using value-of-product data.
**Railway investment in 1840 estimated at 15 million marks
Source: Tilly (1978), 427.

1. A reminder for readers: capital formation, of course, is another name for investment, and net capital formation (or net investment) represented nothing other than changes in the capital stock.

capital stock probably had a structure that approximated the distribution of table 7.

By comparing the above-cited estimates of net investment with available estimates of national product we come up with relatively low "investment rates" for the 1840s, between 5 and 6 percent.[2] This finding raises two questions. One concerns the role of capital formation in industrial growth: do relatively low investment rates mean that the presumed acceleration of industrial growth in the 1840s had little to do with capital formation? The other question that deserves more reflection is whether investment rates in general and industrial investment in particular were low because the supply of capital was low or because the demand for capital was weak. Basically, this reduces to the question of the supply of financial capital relative to the investment demand—a question that has been hotly debated in the German economic historiography.[3] Suffice it to say here that much evidence points to a more than adequate aggregate supply of finance before 1850, indicated, for example, by reference to a small number of individual fortunes, each of which were larger than the total capital stock of the most

Table 7: Estimated Stock of Capital and Net Investment in Germany in 1850 (in millions of marks, current prices)

	Capital Stock	Net Investment
Agriculture	15,900	30
Housing	4,750	140
Public buildings	1,230	30
Railways	970	300
Other infrastructure	3,730	40
Industry and trade	5,830	30
Total	**32,400**	**570**

Source: W. Hoffmann, *Das Wachstum der deutschen Wirtschaft seit der Mitte des 19. Jahrhunderts* (Berlin and Heidelberg, N.Y., 1965), tables 40 and 42.

2. The national product data are for Germany and are taken from R. Spree, *Wachstumszyklen der deutschen Wirtschaft, 1840–1880* (Berlin, 1977). They are projected to Prussia on the basis of the estimates of W. Hoffmann and J. Müller, *Das deutsche Volkseinkommen, 1851–1957* (Tübingen, 1959), 39–40 and 86–87.

3. The locus classicus of this debate is doubtless K. Borchardt, "Die Frage des Kapitalmangels in der ersten Hälfte des 19. Jahrhunderts in Deutschland," in *Wachstum, Krisen, Handlungsspielräume der Wirtschaftspolitik. Studien zur Wirtschaftsgeschichte des 19. und 20. Jahrhunderts*, ed. K. Borchardt, Kritische Studien zur Geschichtswissenschaft 50 (Göttingen, 1982), 28–41.

important German industries of the time, or by the falling rates of interest and evidence of capital exports from Germany in the 1830s and early 1840s.[4] Such evidence points to the conclusion that industrial investment in Germany in this earlier period reflected weak demands, rather than inadequate supplies of financial capital. It is quite likely that industrial investment involved high risks, some of which were inherent in the early phases of industrialization and had nothing to do with finance. Which is not to say, however, that finance—and financial capital—did not matter. But as suggested in chapter 3, it probably mattered much more for infrastructural investment than it did for industry.

Labor Force

Labor in general is and was the most important input in the economy. And the growth of wage labor was certainly one of the most important factors contributing to Germany's economic expansion in the nineteenth century.

In turning to the main features of labor force development in nineteenth-century Germany (and focusing particular attention on the period before 1850), we do not imply that wage labor originated at this time. There is no doubt that wage labor existed long before the nineteenth century. The Bible records the existence of workers in the vineyard, who were paid wages daily and hired on a daily basis. Wage laborers also worked in craft trades, and, in addition to slaves, formed a large part of the agricultural work force. In the Middle Ages, craftmasters hired many wage laborers who never became masters on their own. Wage labor as a form of labor organization did exist, but it did not dominate before the modern period. In Germany, according to a semi-official Zollverein estimate, wage earners amounted to no more than 20 percent of the total workforce in 1846. In the following decades, however, their numbers increased dramatically, concentrating disproportionately in urban centers and fed by migration from rural areas—of laborers from dying rural industries, agricultural subsistence workers, small landholders—and from centers of traditional craft industries.[5] In the following pages, we attempt to

---

4. See, in addition to Borchardt (1982), B. Brockhage, *Zur Entwicklung des preussisch-deutschen Kapitalexports* (Leipzig, 1910).
5. See F.-W. Henning, *Das vorindustrielle Deutschland* (Paderborn, 1977), 265.

describe how the forms of labor organization developed in the early nineteenth century. We begin with the case of agriculture, despite all of its idiosyncratic features.

Labor in Agriculture

Agriculture dominated the German economy until well past the 1850s. In 1816, 80 percent of the Prussian population lived in the countryside, but by 1858 the share had fallen to 45 percent, even though it remained stable in absolute numbers.[6] Table 8 depicts this development.

Employment shares tell a somewhat different story, for in the early nineteenth century no more than 65 percent of the population worked primarily in agriculture, while some 20 percent were in trade and commerce and 15 percent in the service sector. Some of the discrepancy (between the 80 percent of rural residents and the 65 percent of the table) is related to the presence of rural industry, a point to which we shall return. Employment shares are not the same thing as absolute numbers. Over the nineteenth century the agricultural labor force grew substantially in absolute terms. Our graph 6 reproduces two estimates for the state of Prussia and for Germany as a whole.

Readers will note that the series presented here have gaps, and these reflect the fact that occupation and employment censuses were not carried out every year. The series "Prussia" and "Germany" are based on the research work of Gertrud Helling, the series "Germany" on the work of Walther Hoffmann. Differences

Table 8: Share of Rural Population in Prussia (total and percent of total population)

Year	Rural Population		Non-rural Population	
	Total (in millions)	% of total population	Total (in millions)	% of total population
1816	18.48	80.00	4.62	20.00
1858	16.12	45.41	19.38	54.59

Source: H. J. Teuteberg, *Die deutsche Landwirtschaft beim Eintritt in die Phase der Hochindustrialisierung* (Cologne, 1977), 21.

6. H. J. Teuteberg, *Die deutsche Landwirtschaft beim Eintritt in die Phase der Hochindustrialisierung* (Cologne, 1977).

Graph 6: The Growth of the Agricultural Labor Force in Prussia and Germany (1800–1913) (in thousands)

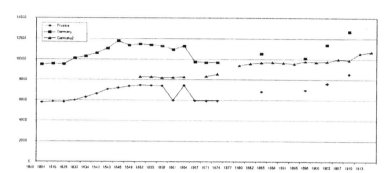

between Helling and Hoffmann are the result of different treatment of the sub-categories self-employed and family members.[7] The Hoffmann series is actually an annual one from 1875 on, but the between-census estimates are interpolations. Note the shift in the 1860s and resurgence of growth since 1871. This partly reflects redefinition of the agricultural labor force to include female family members; but it also reflects population growth and the general tenacity of agriculture as a source of income in Germany. And that is the main point we wish to stress here. All of the series do reflect the long-run positive growth trend of the agricultural labor force, and this, in turn, reflects (a) the growing German population and possibly also (b) the continuing attractiveness of family-based agriculture.

Nevertheless, the series in graph 6 are aggregate estimates covering a long period of time. In fact, the labor force situation in the early phases of industrialization was a highly differentiated one. The kinds of tasks actually performed by agricultural laborers depended on their place in the stratified society in which they lived. Interesting information on that stratification can be found in the work of such scholars as Ziekursch, Krug, or Henning.[8] Thus,

7. Interested readers are referred to Hoffmann (1965), 180–206; and also to G. Helling, "Zur Entwicklung der Produktivität in der deutschen Landwirtschaft im 19. Jahrhundert," in *Jahrbuch für Wirtschaftsgeschichte* 1 (1966): 129–41, here 140.

8. For an assessment of the relevant sources, see F. W. Henning, "Die Betriebsgrößenstruktur der mitteleuropäischen Landwirtschaft im 18. Jahrhundert und ihr

for rural Prussian society at the turn of the eighteenth to the nineteenth century, we find that independent peasants (*Bauern*)—that is, persons who disposed over sufficient land to support a family—represented only a minority of the population. As a percentage of the total population they represented 42 percent in East Prussia, 35 percent in Pomerania, 26 in Brandenburg, 21 in Paderborn in Westphalia, 8 in Silesia, and 39 percent in Prussia as a whole. Most of the rural population had only limited access to land. Sometimes they possessed small plots, sometimes nothing at all. In essence it was this limitation which ensured that a substantial share of the rural population did, in fact, have to work for others. Some of them worked as craftsmen (perhaps 5 to 6 percent), most of them at least part of the time as rural laborers, in various occupations determined by their positions in the hierarchy of rural society. Our tables 9a and 9b, which draw on estimates made for the late eighteenth century, can give a rough idea of the kinds of differences which existed at the beginning of our period. Two tables are offered in order to cover two somewhat differing classification schemas.

Table 9a: Rural Social Structure in Prussia in the Eighteenth Century (in percent)

	East Prussia	in %	Middle and Farther Pomerania	in %	Brandenburg	in %	Principality Paderborn	in %
Peasants and semi-peasants	Landholders (35–40 ha)	42	Landholders (10–20 ha)	35	Landholders	26	Large and small landholders	21
	Cottage-holders	12	"Half"-land-holders and and cottagers (2–9 ha)	4	Cottage-holders	14	Cottagers	51
Landless	Cottagers	35	Cottagers (up to 3 ha)	23	Cottagers	15	–	–
	Shepherds	6	Shepherds	6	Shepherds	6	Shepherds	6
	Craftsmen	5	Craftsmen	6	Craftsmen	6	–	–
	–	–	Other*	26	Other*	33	Other*	22
Total		100		100		100		100

*In German, "Einlieger" (rent-paying tenants of peasant landowners).

Source: F. W. Henning, "Die Betriebsgrößenstruktur der mitteleuropäischen Landwirtschaft im 18. Jahrhundert und ihr Einfluß auf die ländlichen Einkommensverhältnisse," in *Zeitschrift für Agrargeschichte und Agrarsoziologie* 17 (1969): 171–93.

Einfluß auf die ländlichen Einkommensverhältnisse," *Zeitschrift für Agrargeschichte und Agrarsoziologie* 17 (1969): 171–93.

Table 9b: Rural Social Structure in Prussia and Silesia

	Silesia (1770)	Total	in %	Prussia (1805)	Total	in %
Peasants and semi-peasants	Landholders	40–50,000	7.8	Landholders	401,000	39.0
	Cottageholders	140–150,000	25.2	–	–	–
Landless	Other*	30–40,000	6.0	Cottageholders	350,000	34.0
	Servants	350,000	60.0	Landless	282,000	28.0
Total		575,000	100.0		1,033,000	100.0

*In German, "Einlieger" (rent-paying tenants of peasant landowners).

Source: J. Kocka, *Weder Stand noch Klasse, Unterschichten um 1800* (Bonn, 1990), 85.

The tables deserve some commentary. First, as previously noted in our text, regional differences in social structure—and hence in the extent of wage labor—were pronounced.

Second, a part of the differences observable here reflect different ways of counting. In table 9b, for example, the great weight of domestic employment (servants) recorded for Silesia obscures the fact that this represented a life-cycle-dependent status, itself dependent in turn on the age distribution of the rural population. Strictly speaking, it is not comparable with the category village landless recorded here for Prussia. The basic message of the tables is that agricultural labor in the early nineteenth century was still far from representing a purely labor market phenomenon, determined by aggregate supply, demand, and market prices. Part-time work and partial self-employment were still dominant factors affecting the agricultural labor force at this stage.

By the 1850s, some changes were becoming evident. Table 10 offers a picture of the agricultural social structure around sixty years later than the date underlying tables 9a and 9b.

Thus, by 1861, after the agrarian reforms described in the previous chapter had largely run their course, over half of the agricultural population represented self-employed landholders, farmers or estate managers (and their family members), while only 12.8 percent, or about one-eighth were officially classifiable as wage laborers. It is quite likely, to be sure, that the category of "part-time farmers" represented a group in need of supplementary income that would have led to at least part-time employment and wage labor. Moreover, at roughly the same time (1858) around 15,000 large landowners held over half of the cultivable land in Prussia, while some 300,000 owners held only very small plots.

Table 10: Social Structure of Agricultural Population in Prussia (1861)

Social Status	East Elbian Provinces		Prussian State, Total	
	Number	Percent	Number	Percent
Landowners, farmers, estate managers (incl. family)	2,575,014	51.3	4,294,152	51.1
Part-time farmers (incl. family)	1,065,318	21.2	1,892,224	22.5
Servants, domestic help*	744,923	14.7	1,072,150	12.7
Day laborers, unskilled laborers	638,930	12.8	1,140,642	13.6
Total	5,024,185	100.0	8,399,730	100.0

*Excluding family members.

Sources: G. von Viebahn, *Statistik des nördlichen und zollvereinten Deutschlands*, vol. 2 (Berlin, 1862), 585, 604; Königlich Preussisches Statistisches Büro, *Preussische Statistik*, vol. 4 (Berlin, 1864).

This represented a distribution that doubtless encouraged the employment of wage labor (large landowners employing family members of smallholders). Nevertheless, the judgement applied above to the beginning of the nineteenth century also applies to the 1860s: agricultural labor relations were far from being a pure market result, but were still powerfully influenced by institutional factors such as land tenures.

Labor in Industry and Handicrafts

During the entire first half of the nineteenth century, the population of Germany expanded at a fast pace. This phenomenon lay behind the ongoing growth of the agricultural labor force, as noted above, and it greatly influenced the development of the labor market. At the aggregate level, one can say that the labor force potential grew faster than the number of jobs.[9] Under the circumstances of the times, this disequilibrium situation did not lead to open unemployment, but to what we may term "disguised unemployment" i.e., it took the form of movements of workers into lower-level jobs and into part-time employment (including self-employment). The "secondary sector," which we can divide into handicrafts, rural domestic industry, and manufacturing, was also affected by population growth. Table 11 shows the estimated distribution of employment across these three categories around

9. W. Köllmann, "Bevölkerung und Arbeitspotential in Deutschland 1815–1865," in *Bevölkerung in der industriellen Revolution*, ed. W. Köllmann (Göttingen, 1974), 61–98.

Table 11: Labor in Industry and Handicrafts in Germany around 1800 (in percent and absolute numbers)

Branch	Handi-crafts	Rural Industry	Manufac-turing	Total in %	Absolute Numbers
Metals	5.6	1.0	1.0	7.6	170,000
Building	10.4	0.0	0.0	10.4	240,000
Bricks and clays	2.9	0.0	0.2	3.1	70,000
Mechanics	0.7	0.1	0.1	0.9	20,000
Textile, clothing	8.3	41.0	3.2	52.5	1,170,000
Timber, paper	8.6	1.0	0.7	10.3	230,000
Food	13.4	0.0	0.0	13.4	300,000
Mining	0.0	0.0	1.8	1.8	40,000
Total	49.9	43.1	7.0	100.0	2,240,000

Source: F.-W. Henning, *Das vorindustrielle Deutschland 800 bis 1800* (Paderborn, 1977), 265.

Table 12: Labor in Industry and Handicrafts in Germany around 1850 (in percent and absolute numbers)

Branch	Handi-crafts	Rural Industry	Manufac-turing	Total in %	Absolute Numbers
Metals				9.2	313,000
Building				9.9	337,000
Bricks and clays				4.2	142,000
Mechanics				1.2	40,000
Textile, clothing				48.2	1,638,000
Wood, paper				10.5	356,000
Food and drink				14.5	493,000
Mining				2.8	95,000
Total	46	38	15	100.0	3,400,000

Sources: Henning (1977), 130; Hoffmann (1965), table 15.

1800. It also includes a finer subdivision by branch of industry. Source problems preclude a fully comparable estimate for 1850, but table 12 can suffice for the purpose at hand.

Comparison of the two tables confirms several points. First, growth of secondary employment just about kept in step with population growth (a little over 50 percent). Second, a major shift took place away from domestic industry and handicrafts toward centralized manufacturing (up to over 15 percent). Third, according to Henning (1977), unskilled (or factory-trained) workers grew in importance relative to artisans, whose dominant share reportedly fell from an estimated 75 percent to around two-thirds over the period.[10] This shift reflected, at least in part, the phenomenon of population growth mentioned previously or, to put it differently, the inability of the artisan system to absorb the supply of young workers in search of jobs. Fourth, textiles and clothing remained the largest branch of employment, but its relative importance was declining—in favor of those classic industries of the future, mining, metallurgy and metal-working.

The "industrial" labor force whose growth is documented in the two tables, was far from being homogeneous. This also applies to "wage earners." The group included such diverse types as journeymen in woodworking, miners, foundry workers, day laborers in building and other trades, and domestic servants. Jürgen Kocka provides a comprehensive description of all of these groups in the early nineteenth century.[11] These groups faced different working conditions, and were unevenly distributed over several regions and industries. All in all, they did not resemble Marx's homogeneous and self-confident working class. Quantitative information available to scholars in the early nineteenth century, could provide economists with no more than a rough impression of the "industrial" labor force. According to Kuczynski, the number of "industrial workers" in 1800 barely exceeded 100,000 persons, though for 1816 he estimates around 250,000.[12] Were we to take the category "manufacturing" employment (of tables 11 and 12) as our guide, however, we have an observable increase, between 1800 and 1850, of over 100 percent!

As our tables indicate, rural domestic workers, employed in what has come to be called "proto-industry,"[13] remained an important part of the labor force.[14] It consisted of a specific mixture of industrial and agricultural work involving the rural production of commodities for large-scale traders in supra-regional markets. The work was done at home, mostly by small farmers and

10. Henning (1977), 265. This estimate concerns yet another labor force characteristic—that of skill levels—and derives from Henning (1977), but is not in tables 11 and 12.

11. J. Kocka, *Weder Stand noch Klasse, Unterschichten um 1800* (Bonn, 1990).

12. J. Kuczynski, *Geschichte der Lage der Arbeiter unter dem Kapitalismus*, vol. 1: *Darstellung der Lage der Arbeiter in Deutschland von 1789 bis 1849* (Berlin, 1961), 222.

13. With reference to F. F. Mendels, "Proto-industrialization: The First Phase of the Industrialization Process," *Journal of Economic History* 32 (1972): 241–61.

14. P. Kriedte, H. Medick, and J. Schlumbohm, *Industrialisierung vor der Industrialisierung. Gewerbliche Warenproduktion auf dem Land in der Formationsphase des Kapitalismus* (Göttingen, 1978).

rural laborers seeking additional income. Flax and linen spinning made up most of German textile production, reflecting its close connections to agriculture. The agricultural sector produced the raw materials, but in their free time agricultural workers also spun the yarn and wove the linen. The number of these workers must have been large, for their decline, between around 1850 and 1875, has been estimated at roughly 400,000, more than a quarter of the estimated increase in the entire industrial labor force over the same period.

The gradual, piecemeal industrialization of the labor market in Germany was accompanied by gradual changes in working and living conditions. By current standards, of course, there is much bad news to report on this question: twelve to fourteen hours of work per day were common, as were six-and-a-half day working weeks. It is likely that the standard of living of German workers declined in this early period, particularly in the "hungry forties," although it was to rise later on (see section 2). Declining, or at best stagnating, living standards reflected, at least in part, the rapidly growing population referred to earlier. Most of this growth originated in the countryside, which proved as yet unable to support it. There was therefore much migration to the growing urban centers and many people left Germany entirely and emigrated.[15] All in all, this is evidence of what economists have called a "labor surplus" economy— an economy in which a surplus supply of labor in the traditional sector holds wages in the modernizing sector down, keeping them pretty close to subsistence levels. Though this was seen by contemporaries as a deficiency of early industrialization, the labor surplus could later turn out to be an advantage, as the increasing industrial demand for labor met an abundant and elastic supply.[16] We might see this as part of Germany's mid-century "growth potential."

Technology and Competition: The Case of the Iron Industry

It is useful to explore this factor of modern economic growth with an international comparison. In table 13 we can see the great gap between Great Britain, the industrial leader of this period, and

15. Pierenkemper (1987).
16. See W. A. Lewis, "Economic Development with Unlimited Supplies of Labour," *The Manchester School* 22 (1954), 139–91; see also Tilly (1990).

Table 13: Production and Consumption per Head of Population in Germany compared with the United Kingdom (UK=100)

Year	Consumption of Coal	Production of			Length of Railways
		Pig Iron	Cotton Yarn	Woolen Yarn	
1820	6	–	–	–	–
1830	7	10	–	15	–
1840	7	8	5	26	24
1850	7	6	7	29	35
1860	10	9	11	34	45
1870	17	16	13	39	53
1880	22	23	13	48	80

Source: Hoffmann (1969), 118.

Germany in terms of the level of production in several key branches. By 1880, however, the gap had narrowed significantly, as Germany began producing the same industrial goods as Great Britain and with very similar technologies.

Generally speaking, there are powerful reasons that favor the examination of technological change by means of a sector approach. For economies are technologically heterogeneous, and do not rely merely on one kind of technology. Moreover, each branch of industry follows a specific pattern of technological development. The automobile industry, for example, expanded greatly with the implementation of the assembly line, which later on provided vital input into the electric and electronic industries. Spinning and weaving multiplied textile productivity, but did not become the technology of choice in agriculture. Casting steel with coal had an important effect on the mining and steel industries, but had no impact on linen production. Most technological improvements are limited to a specific branch of an economy, even though they may have important long-term effects for the economy as a whole, as in the case of the steam engine.

To illustrate this point, let us take a closer look at the case of the iron industry up to the 1850s. The iron industry in Germany was dispersed, without advanced technology, and concentrated at ore mining locations. New techniques were imported from Britain and adapted to traditional industrial methods: Specifically, iron ore was melted in a blast furnaced by coke. The pig iron that was produced was "puddled"—a process which reduced the amount of impurities and made the iron more malleable. The puddled iron was then rolled into bars in roll mills. The new techniques blended in with older methods, so that both methods—the wholly new

British technology and the technology mix of old and new in Germany—were roughly equal in efficiency in producing iron and could co-exist for about half a century.[17]

The creation of a modern iron industry, however, soon became a question of capital and organization as well as one of sufficient demand. The traditional methods of production had always satisfied traditional demand, which mainly consisted of ploughs and other agricultural tools. Moreover, tariffs and transportation costs often made the new technologies unprofitable at first. Nonetheless, the new methods were soon integrated into production and developed rapidly, once agriculture and other sectors, driven by new technology, expressed the need for more iron and metal products.

These developments were powerfully affected by the competition of the British industry, which dominated world production and exports of iron over the period (until around the 1870s). The British owed their position to the use of coke or pit coal as smelting fuel, to the production of pig iron, and to the refining of iron by puddling and rolling. Pig and bar iron dominated the international markets. Undoubtedly, British producers supplied the cheapest iron available, though countries protected their own iron producers by imposing tariffs and transportation duties on British iron. The bulk of British iron exports consisted of pig and bar iron as well as railway iron (until 1855). The total British export increased more than tenfold from 1821 to 1850, rising from 33,991 tons to 449,505 tons. The figure for pig iron exports show an increase from 4,552 to 143,731 tons, an even more substantial improvement.

The British sold their iron first and foremost to the U. S., which bought between 10 and 50 percent of total British iron output. France was Britain's second most important market, purchasing large amounts of pig iron in the early nineteenth century. French demand, however, decreased considerably around mid-century. On the other hand, France imported only small amounts of bar iron. The Netherlands—with included Belgium until 1830—also imported a great deal of British pig iron, but much less bar iron. The various German states, meanwhile, required little iron in the early nineteenth century, though their demand expanded from the 1840s on.

17. Rainer Fremdling, "Foreign Competition and Technological Change: British Exports and the Modernization of German Iron Industry from the 1820s to the 1860s," in *German Industry and German Industrialization*, ed. W. R. Lee (London, 1991), 47–76.

Domestically produced German iron proved unable to meet the demands of consumers in the early nineteenth century because of insufficient resources, technological obsolescence, high prices, and high production costs. British competition had conflicting effects. On the one hand it inhibited German production and delayed the growth of the German iron-industry. On the other hand, British imports helped speed the diffusion of new technologies, and promoted long-term modernization of coked pig iron and puddled and rolled bar iron. Thus, the iron trade paved the way for the transfer of technology. German iron producers borrowed selectively from the British model, and adopted only parts of the new technologies so as to blend them with traditional techniques.

Some examples might illustrate the partial integration of new technologies: German iron masters adopted the coal furnace, but not the steam engine, which the British used to produce a high-pressure blast. They also combined the blast furnace with traditional water mills, which worked quite well for a while. While hot blasts—blasts into a furnace heated by smelting—were originally invented in Britain as part of the modern coke-blast-furnace, German iron masters applied this new technology to traditional charcoal furnaces.

The German iron industry developed in a relatively continuous fashion up until 1843–44. Prices remained stable while production recorded slight to moderate increases. German railway construction, meanwhile, began on a small-scale basis in 1835, then boomed, giving rise to an exceptional development of demand which could not be met by domestic producers alone. A third of all iron production and a quarter of all consumption derived from railway construction. (Pig iron equivalents make pig and bar iron statistically comparable. Bar iron contains a certain amount of pig iron, from which bar iron is produced.)

It was this rising demand for iron that forced German iron masters to adopt the new technologies. They did so successfully. Gradually, domestic production displaced imported iron. In 1843, for example, only 10 percent of all German rail was produced domestically. Twenty years later, over 85 percent was manufactured domestically. Without a doubt, this impressive increase in domestic production was tied to technological innovations and the resulting modernization of the German iron industry.

Production statistics for Prussia permit comparison of iron produced by traditional means with that produced with the new technologies. In 1837, only 10 percent of Prussian pig iron was produced with mineral fuel, whereas over 90 percent was still produced with charcoal. By 1850, the percentage produced using charcoal had dropped to 75 percent, which was still considerable. Five years later, however, this figure had fallen to 50 percent. During the 1860s, coal finally replaced charcoal as an element in the smelting process, and plant fuel became obsolete.

In bar iron production, the substitution of traditional with modern modes of production can be observed much earlier. As early as 1836, nearly one-third (32.1 percent) of all bar iron was produced from mineral fuel. This amount increased rapidly, so that ten years later half of all bar iron was produced with coke or pit-coal. During the 1850s, charcoal almost disappeared as an element in bar iron production. In this way, the substitution of plant to mineral fuel was complete, symbolizing the acceptance of new technologies and a successful import-substitution.

German tariff policies and the creation of the Zollverein also influenced German iron imports. Pig iron, classified as raw material, remained exempt from duty until 1843. Prussian iron tariffs protected domestic bar iron and consisted of duties on bar iron and rail products. In contrast to bar iron tariffs the 1843 tariff on pig iron was very moderate, and was not intended to protect the domestic pig iron industry.

After 1850, a dramatic change in the structure of export markets made the U.S. the top purchaser of British iron, with France as an important customer as well. Germany became almost self-sufficient, reducing its imports from countries such as Belgium, and it eventually began to export iron goods to Eastern Europe, Russia, southwestern Europe, Austria, Romania, and to the U.S. In short, Germany became an important international competitor for Britain.

The burgeoning German iron industry offers an interesting case study in the development of modern technology. We might have taken other examples, such as the development of the steam engine, of coal mining, or of the chemical industry, which gave us soda, new dyes, and pharmaceutical goods. Technological change follows particular paths and thus deserves its status as a special field of economic history. As we have tried to show, however, technological change needs to be placed in sectoral context. This is particularly true of the iron industry, which had a key sectoral role to play in the "take-off" phase of German industrial growth—to which we now turn.

Railways and the Leading Sector Syndrome: Backward and Forward Linkages

If we were required to give just one reason why the German iron industry, described in the previous section, grew so rapidly in the 1850s, we would have to say: "railways." That connection will be taken up again here. Railways, however, were also an answer to a broader German problem: its inadequate transportation facilities. In spite of an ambitious Prussian program of road-building and waterway improvements in the 1820s, Germany's transportation system in the 1830s was still in relatively poor shape, far inferior, for example, to that of post-Napoleonic France. This fact alone made the arrival of the railroads an event of great consequence for Germany's economic history, more so, perhaps, than for any other European country. In Germany, as capital was readily available, the rail networks were built rapidly, and large volumes of profitable traffic developed almost immediately. By 1845, Germany was in possession of a larger railway system than France (see table 14).

It is for these reasons that economic historians have assigned railways a crucial role in German industrialization. They were a "leading sector" which, by virtue of its rapid growth, its great economic weight, and above all its linkages with the rest of the economy and in particular with heavy industry, markedly influenced the pattern of German industrial development between, say, the 1840s and the 1870s.

Table 14: Additions to the Railway System in Germany (1835–1880) (in kilometers)

Year	Length of system	% in addition
1835	6	–
1840	549	–
1845	2,131	–
1850	5,822	–
1855	7,781	34
1860	11,026	41
1865	13,821	25
1870	18,560	34
1875	27,795	55
1880	33,865	21

Source: Milward and Saul (1977), 380.

The "leading sector" hypothesis of German industrialization turns on three distinctive features about the railways: (1) the timing and nature of railway and heavy industrial investment; (2) the size of railway investment; and (3) the productivity and transport price implications of railway growth. We take up these points in turn.

First, expansion of what we call the "leading sector syndrome" (LSS) resulted from both market forces and state intervention. In Prussia, railway building depended on state approval for several reasons (e.g., land expropriation rights), and it was not until the 1830s that a consistent set of procedures for the concessioning of new lines was developed.[18] This freed railway investment of one important restraint, and it took off in the early 1840s until slowed down in 1844 by a law against "speculative transactions" in railway securities and then stopped by the commercial and financial crisis of 1847–48.[19] The Revolution of 1848–49 which immediately followed that crisis altered the conditions under which the LSS developed, and in two ways: (1) thanks to the stabilized political situation after 1849 the state was willing to pour a much larger volume of financial resources into railways in the 1850s than it had in the 1840s; and (2) the state liberalized its policy toward the chartering of joint-stock industrial companies, and it also withdrew from close administrative control of coal mining.[20] The juncture of these changes permitted a strong promotional and investment boom to take place in German heavy industry in the 1850s—one of the most remarkable economic booms of the entire nineteenth century.[21]

18. On this, see D. Eichholtz, *Junker und Bourgeoisie vor 1848 in der preußischen Eisenbahngeschichte* (Berlin, 1962); J. Brophy, *Capitalism, Politics and Railroads in Prussia, 1830–1870* (Columbus, 1998); R. Fremdling, *Eisenbahnen und deutsches Wirtschaftswachstum 1840–1879* (Dortmund, 1975).

19. On this theme, see J. Bergmann, "Ökonomische Voraussetzungen der Revolution von 1848. Zur Krise von 1845–48 in Deutschland," in *Zweihundert Jahre amerikanische Revolution und moderne Revolutionsforschung*, ed. H.-U. Wehler (Göttingen, 1976), 254–87; H. Kubitschek, "Die Börsenverordnung von 28. Mai 1844 und die Situation im Finanz- und Kreditwesen Preußens in den vierziger Jahren des 19. Jahrhunderts (1840 bis 1847)," *Jahrbuch für Wirtschaftsgeschichte* 4 (1962): 57–78.

20. See W. Fischer, "Die Stellung der preußischen Bergrechtreform von 1851–1865 in der Wirtschafts- und Sozialverfassung des 19. Jahrhunderts," reprinted in W. Fischer, *Wirtschaft und Gesellschaft im Zeitalter der Industrialisierung* (Göttingen, 1972), 148–60; see also H. Blumberg, "Die Finanzierung der Neugründungen und Erweiterungen von Industriebetrieben in Form der Aktiengesellschaften während der fünfziger Jahre des 19. Jahrhunderts in Deutschland, am Beispiel der preußischen Verhältnisse erläutert," in *Studien zur Geschichte der industriellen Revolution in Deutschland*, ed. H. Mottek et al. (Berlin, 1960), 164–208.

21. See H. Rosenberg, *Die Weltwirtschaftskrise 1857–59* (Göttingen, 1974).

It would be misleading, however, to view the expansion of the LSS as an offspring of state action. Against the background of the political shifts just described, market forces largely determined the developmental pattern. For the principal determinant of railroad investment over the period was in all probability expected profits, as measured, for example, by the rate of return on railway investments. Graph 7 reproduces an estimate of the rate of return and juxtaposes it with the rate of growth of the railroads' capital stock—a reflection of railroad investment. The correlation is striking (r = 0.65). Note that these expectations were not irrational, for the returns to capitalists measured here were related to realized revenues, which grew rapidly enough to suggest the presence of an adequate demand for railway services from the outset. Investment in coal and iron, in turn, appears to have depended on their own prices in previous periods and on sales to the railways.[22] What we have, then, is a modern sector responding, not to the real incomes or consumption patterns of the economy as a whole, but to an initially small, but dynamically growing core of interdependent, modern industrial enterprises dominated by profit expectations. The cycles and crises of the 1840s, 1850s, 1860s and 1870s—reflected in the steep declines in the rate of return shown in graph 7—underscore the essentially unplanned market character of this period's development.[23]

Second, railways were highly capital intensive, large-scale enterprises from the very beginning and, as such, soon began to exercise a perceptible influence on the rest of the economy. Their initial construction, and later, their operation, generated incomes and employment, both directly and indirectly. As early as the 1840s contemporary German observers, distressed by the poverty and underemployment around them, advocated railway investment spending as a productive form of poverty relief and job creation. Retrospectively, moreover, it is possible to identify railway investment as the economy's chief "cycle maker," for most of the key indicators of business-cycle movement tended to follow railway investment up and down over the cycles of the period.[24] Table

22. Fremdling (1975); R. Fremdling, "Railroads and German Economic Growth: A Leading Sector Analysis with a Comparison to the United States and Great Britain," *Journal of Economic History* 37 (1977): 583–604; C.-L. Holtfrerich, *Quantitative Wirtschaftsgeschichte des Ruhrkohlenbergbaus im 19. Jahrhundert. Eine Führungssektoranalyse* (Dortmund, 1973); Spree (1977).

23. For a generalization of this interpretation, see Spree (1977).

24. See especially Spree (1977).

Graph 7: Rate of Return on Capital (W_R) and Rates of Growth of Capital Stock (W_{in}) in Prussian Railways (1841–1879)

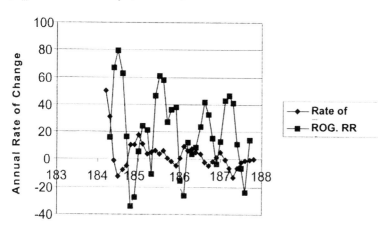

Source: R. Fremdling, *Eisenbahnen und deutsches Wirtschaftswachstum 1840–1879* (Dortmund, 1975), 153.

15 offers one indicator of the weight of railroad investment in the overall German economy of the period. As the table shows, railroad investment could exceed total manufacturing investment at times.

To appreciate the impact of railroads, however, we need to introduce the concept of backward linkages. These show how the railways' demand for inputs influenced the sales, profits, production, and, ultimately, investment in those branches of the economy which supplied such inputs. Analytically, a backward linkage here refers to the additional investment undertaken in an input-supplying branch in response to the railway demand.[25] If we look, for example, at the number of locomotives purchased by Prussian railways in the early period, we find that the first German engine was acquired in 1840. Up to that point, Prussia's locomotives were imported from abroad. From the early 1840s on, however, foreign procurement rapidly diminished (as table 16 shows).

This is a remarkable case of import substitution induced by backward linkages. The growth of the large engineering works (such as

25. The underlying assumption here is that the economy had unemployed resources, with backward-linkage investment having "zero opportunity costs" in the sense that the additional labor and capital employed in industries in response to the railroad demands would have otherwise remained unemployed. This is not implausible for the period in question.

Table 15: Railway Net Investment in Relation to Investment in Manufacturing and in Aggregate in Germany (1851–1879) (annual averages in mill. marks* and percent)

Period	Railway (mill. marks)	Manufacturing (%)	Aggregate Economy (%)
1851–54	88	78.3	11.9
1855–59	134	78.6	19.7
1860–64	142	57.6	11.8
1865–69	201	113.0	17.5
1870–74	425	59.2	18.6
1875–79	503	246.4	25.8

*In current prices.

Sources: Fremdling (1975), 31; and Hoffmann (1965), 259.

Table 16: Distribution of the Locomotives in Prussian Railways by Year of Purchase and Country of Origin in 1853

Year	Total No.	Germany No.	%	Great Britain No.	%	Belgium No.	%	U.S. No.	%
1838	7	0		6	85.7	1	14.3	0	
1839	12	0		12	100.0	0		0	
1840	12	1	8.3	11	91.7	0		0	
1841	20	0		19	95.0	1	5.0	0	
1842	22	6	27.3	12	54.5	2	9.1	2	9.1
1843	35	11	31.4	13	37.1	3	8.6	8	22.9
1844	17	7	41.2	8	47.0	1	5.9	1	5.9
1845	50	26	52.0	21	42.0	3	6.0	0	–
1846	80	56	70.0	20	25.0	4	5.0	0	–
1847	106	72	67.9	14	13.2	20	18.9	0	–
1848	74	57	77.0	11	14.9	6	8.1	0	–
1849	24	23	95.8	0	–	1	4.2	0	–
1850	53	42	79.2	5	9.4	6	11.3	0	–
1851	54	54	100.0	0	–	0		–	–
1852	58	56	96.6	1	1.7	1	1.7	0	–
1853	105	99	94.3	0	–	6	5.7	0	–

Source: R. Fremdling, "Railroads and German Economic Growth: A Leading Sector Analysis with a Comparison to the United States and Great Britain," *Journal of Economic History* 3 (1977): 583–604, here 588.

Borsig in Berlin)[26] in this period clearly owed much to expanding railway demand. Even more important, however, were the key branches of coal mining and iron and steel-making. Economic historians have made some input-output calculations indicating the closeness of these linkages. A rough representation is given in table 17. Note the asymmetry: railways influenced coal and iron much more than they were influenced by the latter. Whereas railroads absorbed over one-third of German iron output in the 1850s, and thus, indirectly, more than 4 percent of coal mining production, both those sectors took no more than 1 percent of railroad output. That is to say, railroad demands were driving the "system." However, it is important to stress the dynamic and qualitative effects. As an example of the former, one may note the difference between the 1840s and the 1850s. In the 1840s, Prussian railways grew at a rate of 20 percent per year, iron and coal at rates of 4 percent and 4.5 percent, respectively. Prussian ironworks helped to supply the expanding railway sector with rails, but most of the supply was imported from abroad, for Prussian and German industry was far too small and backward to meet the huge demand. However, the profits for those who could satisfy part of it were large enough to induce considerable investment in iron and rail-making capacity, and by the 1850s the picture was radically changing. In the 1850s, we observe rates of growth as follows: railways = 10 percent, iron = 30 percent, and coal = 9 percent.

By the 1850s, it can be seen that Prussia had become a net exporter of iron-rails, so thoroughgoing had been the transformation

Table 17: Input-Output Sectoral Relations in Germany in the 1850s (coefficients in percentage of consumption)

Deliveries to: From:	Railroads	Coal Mining	Iron- working	Total Consumption= Production+(Im-Ex)
Railroads		1		
Coal Mining	2	7	12	100=102–2
Ironworking	36			100= 96+4

Source: Adapted from R. Fremdling, "Modernisierung und Wachstum der Schwerindustrie in Deutschland, 1830–1860," *Geschichte und Gesellschaft* 5 (1979): 201–27, he.. 224.

26. R. Thoma, "Der Industriekomplex von A. Borsig. Unternehmensentwicklung von 1837 bis 1932 und betriebswirtschaftliche Analyse unter besonderer Berücksichtigung des oberschlesischen Borsigwerks" (Ph.D. diss., University of Cologne, 2002).

of its industry. This transformation reflects, though does not reveal, qualitative changes. For it is important to add that the largest, most modern iron and steel works by the 1860s were those that had grown by servicing the needs of the railways. Without the railways, the shift from the older charcoal technology to more efficient coke smelting and refining methods would doubtless have taken much longer. Moreover, these were the enterprises that pioneered the industrial use of such organizational forms as the joint-stock company. That was an important step forward in itself.

Railways, we have already noted, mobilized large, unprecedented sums of capital. They did so largely through the banking system. For this reason, development of the latter can be viewed, in a sense, as a backward linkage generated by the former. The development of that particularly German phenomenon of "universal" or "mixed" banking practice, may be traced, at least in part, to the demands of railway finance. At the founding of the first railway companies in the 1830s, in any case, we find private bankers playing an important role. They are members of the organizing committees, they subscribe a significant part of the company's initial share capital, both in their own name and on behalf of their customers. They serve as bankers or fiscal agents of the new companies, supply those companies with working capital, the employment of which they monitor by serving also as directors. Their election to such directorships, in turn, is ensured by their control of proxy shareowners' voting rights at the shareholders' meetings. And they participate in syndicates of bankers formed to finance the railways' chronic needs for additional capital—not infrequently to "fund" the short-term debt run up with bankers—whether in the form of shares, preferred shares, or in fixed-interest bonds. In short, virtually all of the practices which became well known as characteristic of German universal banking in the late nineteenth century were pioneered in Germany's early Railway Age. Indeed, the principal motivation behind the creation of the joint-stock banks, whose growth eventually eclipsed that of the private bankers, derived in strong measure from limits those bankers experienced in financing railways at a time when they themselves had no direct access to the instrument of limited liability.[27] It is important to remember, finally, that the techniques

27. Joint-stock companies such as railroad companies (and later banks) were generally granted limited liability rights. That is, were these companies to incur debts and fail, persons who owned shares of such companies could be made liable

and resources that banks and bankers developed and accumulated in the railway business became available for the finance of other sectors, such as coal, iron and steel, or heavy machinery, when their needs reached appropriate levels.

Forward linkages were also important. These may be formally defined as investments in capacity which were undertaken due to the transportation improvements brought about by railways. We need to recall that railways realized high rates of technological progress and productivity increase almost from their beginnings, partly through economies of scale (more intensive utilization of fixed investment), partly through technical and organizational improvements (standardization of equipment, better scheduling, etc.). Competition for traffic among railway lines ensured that cost savings were passed on to railway users in the form of price reductions. Interestingly, the first railway companies set prices relatively high, apparently assuming an inelastic but sufficient demand for their product.[28] As competition forced prices down, the companies were surprised by the increased revenues that followed—which suggested relatively high elasticity of demand. In a sense, therefore, one might say that cost reductions in railroading coupled to competition generated the observed demand. Graph 8, which shows how freight rates fell after 1840, suggests that the cost savings were substantial.

Ernst Engel, a contemporary observer, compared pre-railway land freight rates with those realized by railways in the 1840–75 period and calculated how much revenue they would have generated at historically observed volumes of traffic. The difference represented the savings that railways made possible, a difference he estimated at roughly 20 billion marks—or more than the cumulative costs of construction up to that time.[29]

---

for no more than the value of those shares. Thus protected, capitalists could be more easily induced to make financial investments in such companies, whose capital base, in turn, could be expanded more readily.

28. The "elasticity of demand" refers to the responsiveness of the quantity of a product demanded to changes in its price. Where demand is "inelastic," price reductions lead to disproportionately low increases in sales and a decline in total revenues (= price x quantity), and in the presence of "elastic" demand price reductions produce increased total revenue. Obviously, entrepreneurs who operated on the assumption of inelastic demand would be most reluctant to experiment with price cutting. See Fremdling (1975), 145–50, for an application of this line of thought to the early stage of German railroad growth.

29. Ernst Engel was one of the most industrious compilers of statistical information on the German economy in the third quarter of the nineteenth century (and

Graph 8: Freight and Passenger Rates on German Railroads (1840–1880) (in marks per ton-kilometer and passenger)

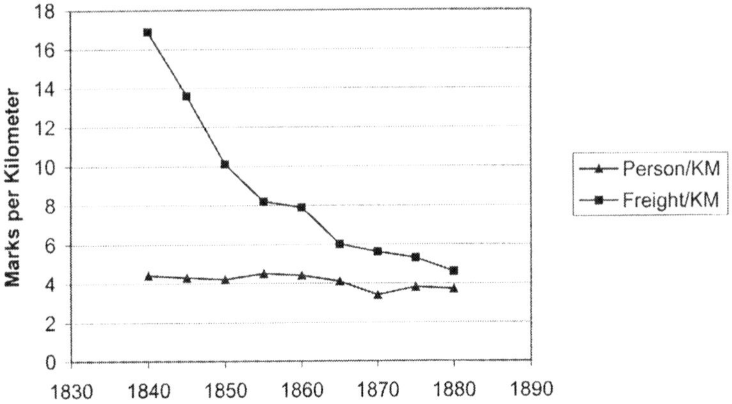

Source: Fremdling (1975), table 23.

The significance of such savings for assessments of railways as a leading sector, however, lies in the forward linkages they might be presumed to have generated among rail transport-using branches: investment and productivity increases which would not have otherwise been realized. We do not know how large these forward linkages were. As a way of suggesting their importance, we look in the following at some concrete instances of railways supplanting waterways. The coal trade offers an instructive example. The fuel consumption of large steel plants in the Saar, the Ruhr valley, Upper Silesia, and Saxony depended on pit coal supplies from nearby coal mining areas. Transportation costs determined whether German coal could compete with British coal or not. Until the middle of the century, high transportation costs kept the sale and distribution of German coal very limited. Thus, around 1840, transportation of coal by cart cost 40 pfennigs for every ton/km, while railways offered between 11 and 14 pfennigs for every ton/km. These coal prices doubled after a journey of 13.5 kilometers (ca. 8 miles) by cart, or after 38–50 kilometers by rail.

---

incidentally also the source of "Engel's Law" on the income elasticity of demand for basic goods). See E. Engel, *Das Zeitalter des Dampfes in technisch-statistischer Beleuchtung* (Separate printing of *Zeitschrift des königlich preussischen statistischen Bureaus 1879*) (Berlin, 1879).

As a result, British coal completely dominated coal trade in northern and central Germany, because the British where able to undercut German transportation costs by shipping British coal by water. In Germany, high costs hindered the long-distance distribution of domestic coal. Cheaper train rates were unavailable for some parts of the country since, for example, Berlin had no rail connections with the Ruhr and Upper Silesia until after 1845. However, Prussian train freight grew from 1 percent in 1850 to 14 percent of all freight ten years later. Coal transportation, facilitated by special train rates, accounts for much of this rise.

Such special "Einpfennig" rates served the interest of the Prussian coal industry, some of which was owned by the Prussian State, and allowed it to face British competition more effectively. Again a process of import substitution took place, as shown in table 18. On the local coal market in Berlin, for example, German coal, which was transported by train, gradually replaced British coal, which was transported by boat. In addition, railways created new markets— in Berlin after 1845, or in Southern Germany somewhat later—and therefore, new demand for coal. Coal from the Saarland found new markets in Bavaria, Baden, and Wuerttemberg after 1850.

Table 18: Coal Transportation to Berlin

	1846	1860	1862	1865	1871	1881
British pit coal						
(1,000s) of metric tons	95	203	181	134	247	75
Market share in %	100	57.4	41.9	20.6	23.0	4.9
of which transportation						
by ship in %	100	98.9	99.9	99.9	100	99.6
Upper Silesian pit coal						
(1,000s) of metric tons	–	66	139	352	562	769
Market share in %	–	18.5	32.1	53.9	52.4	49.8
of which transportation by						
railway in %	–	85.1	99.9	100	99.1	99.9
Total of metric tons (1,000s)	95	354	432	652	1,073	1,546
of which transportation by						
railway in %	0	23.0	47.3	72.9	72.4	92.0

Note: The total includes Bohemian and other German pit coal and lignite.

Source: Fremdling (1975), 62–63.

Finally, to return to a point made earlier, Germany's geography—particularly its lack of major East-West waterways—doubtless enhanced the importance of railways as a modernizing force. It is hard to conceive of a hypothetically modernized canal and river transportation system that could have been a close substitute for the railway system. This fact, taken together with the important backward linkages already discussed, offer strong justification for placing the LSS in the center of our explanation of how and why German industrial growth accelerated so markedly in the third quarter of the nineteenth century.

The Role of the State

We have dwelt at some length on the role of the railways, in part because their development is well documented, a fact that is related, among other things, to their great political importance. As such, their history is inseparable from the role of the state and government policy. The role of the state, already discussed above in connection with the question of institutional preconditions was a factor that may be said to have influenced "the emergence of a modern economy," the subject of this chapter. We therefore offer a brief general discussion of the role of the state at this point, limiting our focus to the pre-1870 period.

A general discussion of the topic is worthwhile because, apart from its objective significance, the role of the state in German industrialization has long held a prominent place in German economic historiography. That is to say, its treatment also allows us to discuss how historians have helped shape our views of the past. We begin by pointing out that the very birth of the discipline of economic history in Germany stemmed from the worries of contemporaries about the social consequences of industrialization in the last quarter of the nineteenth century. Gustav von Schmoller, one of the architects of the so-called "historical school of economics," is the name that springs to mind most readily, for his work and influence reflected the view that liberal economic policies had pernicious effects upon social stability—as Karl Marx had argued—and his research program was oriented toward this problem. Oversimplifying somewhat, we may evaluate this intellectual program as an attempt to use economic history to influence contemporary policies by demonstrating (a) the shortcomings of an unregulated market economy—"Manchester Liberalism" was the label these critics used—and, by implication, (b) the benefits of government intervention in the economy. In what follows, we take a look at two corresponding historiographical consequences.

The first one was a set of attacks on the presumed excessive economic liberalism of the Prussian reform bureaucracy of the Stein-Hardenberg era (roughly 1800–1825). This was the thrust of the celebrated work by a follower of Schmoller, Georg Friedrich Knapp, whose study of the agrarian reforms interpreted peasant emancipation (*Bauernbefreiung*) primarily as the main cause of the rise of a rural, landless proletariat in Prussia.[30] Schmoller himself examined the development of handicraft producers, seeing the Prussian reforms that weakened the craft guilds (e.g., the occupational freedom law of 1810) as a step that accelerated proletarization of craft labor. Some fifty years later, the tradition was still strong. Treue's (1937) study of Prussian reform policies in the critical 1815–25 period attempted to show, with ample documentation, how the advent of liberal commercial policies in Prussia at this time contributed to the destruction of traditional crafts and industries and hindered the development of new ones. This message was picked up by other historians as well (a survey is in Tilly [1968]).[31]

A second particular historiographical result of the same intellectual tradition surfaced in the 1950s and 1960s, along with a strong interest in long-run economic growth. Quite a number of studies began to see state policies as a positive influence upon economic growth. The Prussian State was rehabilitated, e.g., in the literature on state-sponsored technology and skilled worker imports from England, summarized in W. O. Henderson's work.[32] This work also emphasized how technical education was furthered by the establishment of institutions such as the Gewerbe-Institut in Berlin, a precursor of the technical college; and it also praised the Prussian minister Rother, for his use of the Prussian State Bank, the Seehandlung, to finance industrial pilot projects, e.g., in Silesia. U. P. Ritter (1960) drew on this and other literature to summarize Prussian state policy as a case in government promotion of economic development where market forces were as yet too weak

---

30. Georg F. Knapp (1887); Hartmut Harnisch (1984).

31. W. Treue, *Wirtschaftszustände und Wirtschaftspolitik in Preussen 1815–1825* (Stuttgart, 1937); R. Tilly, "Los von England. Probleme des Nationalismus in der deutschen Wirtschaftsgeschichte," *Zeitschrift für das gesamte Staatswissenschaft* 124 (1968): 179–96.

32. W. O. Henderson, *The State and the Industrial Revolution in Prussia, 1740–1870* (Liverpool, 1958).

to ensure success.[33] State subsidization of railway building also received credit as an important development impulse.[34] More recently, Brose has pointed out that the German and Prussian State did not follow a consistent and clear policy with respect to technology.[35] Detailed research on the Prussian case, for example, shows that varying motives underlay technology policies. Thus, the King and other traditional elitist groups represented a species of retrogressive policies, while reformers in the Ministry of Trade and around Beuth also faced pockets of resistance and the need to overcome conflicting motives, for instance those embodied in the administration of mining, the army, or the Prussian State Bank (the Seehandlung) around Christian Rother. The clash of interests among the state bureaucracies became particularly apparent in the nascent iron and steel industry, where complete privatization was looming ahead after 1808. These different interests led to regionally diverging consequences; for example, the continuation of state-run iron and steel works in Upper Silesia, whereas the state-run iron and steel works in the Saar region were privatized.

It would be misleading, however, to speak of a historiographical consensus here. On the one hand, praise of the state and criticism of "the market" is only one strain in the literature, which also contains much of the reverse genre, i.e., criticism of the role of the state and of government policies. There is now quite general acknowledgement that governmental entrepreneurial activity in some areas, e.g., in mining, investment banking, or textiles, may well have been sub-optimal in the sense that it held back potentially more valuable private initiatives.[36] Prussia's railway policies are another area in which the alleged positive effects have been questioned and negative effects on private investment have been registered.[37] On the other hand, in recent years we see an increasing historiographical consciousness on the need to differentiate, i.e., to distinguish between spheres of the economy where government action is essential, and those where it is inappropriate, or at best,

33. U. P. Ritter, *Die Rolle des Staates in den Frühstadien der Industrialisierung. Die preussische Industrieförderung in der ersten Hälfte des 19. Jahrhunderts* (Berlin, 1961).
34. K. Borchard, *Staatsverbrauch und öffentliche Investitionen in Deutschland 1780–1850* (Göttingen, 1968).
35. E. D. Brose, *The Politics of Technological Change in Prussia: Out of the Shadow of Antiquity, 1809–1848* (Princeton, 1993).
36. Borchardt (1973).
37. Fremdling (1975).

inefficient. The production of "public goods" such as justice, peace, and stability corresponds to the former. It thus makes sense to see the Prussian Stein-Hardenberg reforms as providing an institutional framework that secured property rights, thus reducing the costs of economic transactions between the private economic agents affected.[38] The establishment of the German Zollverein may be seen as another such example, since there was no plausible private substitute for the inter-governmental agreements upon which it rested. The Zollverein represented, thanks to the considerable diplomatic investment involved, a credible commitment to reduce interregional trade barriers which almost certainly stimulated capital accumulation and growth.[39] The same can be argued, finally, for Prussian monetary and financial policy, since, as we have seen, the state's obvious commitment to a stable monetary standard will have reduced the perceived riskiness of private financial transactions, at least in the early post-reform period.

In sum, we may agree that "the role of the state" was an important element of German economic development in the early and middle decades of the nineteenth century; but we can also agree, with our historical hindsight, that some "mistakes" were made: the state did too much of some things at times (e.g., the Seehandlung's Silesian investments);[40] and it restricted too much of others (e.g., private banks of issue). It is impossible, however, to draw up a general balance sheet of "costs" and "benefits," as the quantitative basis is still missing. Perhaps it always will be. For the subject involves at least two inherent difficulties, to which, in closing, we would like to refer. First, there is a "natural" source bias in favor of state activity: the overwhelming majority of source materials have to do with governmental actions or governmental surveillance of private ones. Such a distribution may well produce greater historical awareness of the role of the state than of the contribution of the thousands of individual agents and private transactions embodied in "market forces." Entrepreneurial or business history offers a useful corrective, but it is limited—both in quantity and in degree of

38. R. Tilly, "'Perestroika à la Prusse': Preussens liberale Reformen zu Anfang des 19. Jahrhunderts im Lichte des Transformationsparadigmas," *Jahrbuch für Wirtschaftsgeschichte* 2 (1996): 147–60; C. Wischermann, "Der Property Rights-Ansatz und die 'neue' Wirtschaftsgeschichte," *Geschichte und Gesellschaft* 19 (1993): 239–58.

39. Dumke (1984).

40. W. Radtke, *Die Preußische Seehandlung zwischen Staat und Wirtschaft in der Frühphase der Industrialisierung* (Berlin, 1981).

representativeness.[41] Second, the state encompassed a broad range of functions and doubtless affected the economy in myriad ways, most of which had nothing to do with the specific goal of promoting economic development. Increased military spending, for instance, may have boosted aggregate demand in the economy at times, and, in the presence of underemployed resources, economic growth as well. Indeed, the government's overall budget could have frequently had a greater economic impact than specific developmental measures, though unintended.[42] But what about the economic consequences of the introduction of compulsory military service as opposed to its professional alternative? It could take a historian's lifetime to answer such questions adequately. Given the measurement problems, we expect historians to ignore such questions; but still they do involve the state. These points, we conclude, are good grounds for skepticism concerning the claim that the development of the German economy in the early stages of industrialization owed much to the role of the state.

41. T. Pierenkemper, *Unternehmensgeschichte. Eine Einführung in ihre Methoden und Ergebnisse* (Stuttgart, 2000).

42. Economic historians have occasionally examined this particular connection, which is in principle measurable, though with difficulty. See Borchard (1968) for some discussion of the budgetary data of German states as around 1850.

Part Two

THE GERMAN ECONOMY SINCE THE MIDDLE OF THE NINETEENTH CENTURY

Chapter Five

AGRICULTURE

Agriculture represented the largest sector of the German economy in terms of employment, production and investment. By mid-century it was already beginning to resemble a "capitalist" system of production, with well-defined property rights, "free-market" labor relations, and a capitalist-minded class of farmers (or agricultural entrepreneurs). This pattern of development continued over the second half of the nineteenth century, accompanied by important changes in agricultural production.[1]

Such changes in agricultural production contributed powerfully to the modernization of the whole of German society, helping to transform it from an agrarian into an industrial society.[2] As we have seen, the transition had already begun earlier in the nineteenth century, and even had roots in the eighteenth century, such as modern methods introduced by tenant farmers on Prussian Royal Domain Lands, or even Austria's unsuccessful attempt at peasant emancipation under Joseph II. Though certain institutional features of traditional agrarian society survived into the twentieth century, their importance as a determinant of agricultural development declined. They are therefore less interesting for our purposes here than two other, more modern-looking aspects: (1) agricultural improvements in production and productivity; and (2) the role of protective tariffs imposed on agricultural goods.

---

1. J. A. Perkins, "The Agricultural Revolution in Germany," *Journal of European Economic History* 1 (1981): 71–118.

2. This issue of the transformation of state and society was discussed intensively at the end of the century. Cf. A. Wagner, *Agrar- oder Industriestaat* (Jena, 1901); compare also K. D. Barkin, *The Controversy over German Industrialization 1890–1902* (Chicago, 1970).

Production and Productivity

Agricultural production in the first half of the nineteenth century expanded primarily thanks to an increase in productive acreage. Between 1815 and 1849, grain acreage in Prussia expanded by more than 70 percent, from 7.3 million hectares to 12.46 million hectares. By 1864, that figure had reached a total of 14.07 million hectares.[3] This expansion of tilled land was possible in light of a reduction in waste land and a reduction of acreage used for meadows and pasture.

Productivity in the agricultural sector increased at a slow pace in this early period, with production per hectare increasing only moderately. Between 1800 and 1848–52, the principal grain crops registered the increases shown in table 19.[4]

From the same sources, we learn that German agricultural expansion in the early nineteenth century was primarily "factor-intensive"—meaning that it resulted from the greater use of inputs.[5] Those inputs included expanded acreage, labor, and capital. Thus, German agriculture in the early nineteenth century followed traditional forms of expansion without remarkable gains in productivity. It was industrialization rather than anything else which brought qualitative improvements and an increase in productivity to German agriculture, reflected in the acceleration of agricultural output growth after 1850. Roughly comparable figures show the difference (table 20).

Table 19: Output per Hectare of Grain Crops
(1800 to 1848–52)

	Increase in %
Wheat	19
Rye	19
Barley	38
Oats	60

3. G. Franz, "Landwirtschaft 1800–1850," in *Handbuch der deutschen Wirtschafts- und Sozialgeschichte*, ed. H. Aubin and W. Zorn, vol. 2 (Stuttgart, 1976), 276–320, here 309.

4. Ibid., 308.

5. T. Pierenkemper, "Der Agrarsektor in der vorindustriellen Gesellschaft. Einige Anmerkungen zur preußischen Entwicklung 1815–1830 aus produktionstheoretischer Sicht," *Zeitschrift für Agrargeschichte und Agrarsoziologie* 2 (1982): 168–86.

Table 20: Crop Output per Hectare (1849–55 to 1910–13) (increase in percent)

Crop	Rate of Increase	Annual Rate of Increase
Wheat	120	2.00
Rye	125	2.08
Barley	100	1.67
Oats	130	2.17
Potatoes	133	2.22

Source: W. Hoffmann, *Das Wachstum der deutschen Wirtschaft seit der Mitte des 19. Jahrhunderts* (Berlin and Heidelberg, N.Y., 1965), table 49.

Graph 9 reproduces an estimate of crop and animal production for the entire nineteenth century and includes an estimate of the cultivated land area as well.

The slowdown in the growth of the cultivated land area in the 1870s is apparent, and though it was briefly matched by the slowdown in crop production, the subsequent upward trend of the latter and the continuing growth of animal production is unmistakable. Other sources corroborate this picture. Taking agriculture as a whole and viewing the entire period from 1850 to 1913 we have the following estimates of growth:[6]

Output (value added in 1913 prices): 2.28 percent per annum
Cultivated Land: 0.23 percent per annum
Persons Employed: 0.44 percent per annum
Capital Stock: 1.59 percent per annum

Many factors contributed to this improvement in agricultural productivity. Five of these deserve particular attention.

1. The continuing replacement of the old three-field fallow system, in which one of three fields on a given plot of land was left fallow each year in order to spare it and preserve its productivity. The replacement of that system by a more intensive pattern of crop rotation allowed for a larger harvest every year, raising output on the average by about one-third and permitting, obviously, a remarkable increase in productivity per hectare.[7]

6. Taken from W. Hoffmann, *Das Wachstum der deutschen Wirtschaft seit der Mitte des 19. Jahrhunderts* (Berlin and Heidelberg, N.Y., 1965), tables 20, 29, 39, 48, 59.
7. A. S. Milward and S. B. Saul, *The Economic Development of Continental Europe 1780–1870* (London, 1977), 361–94.

Graph 9: Agricultural Production

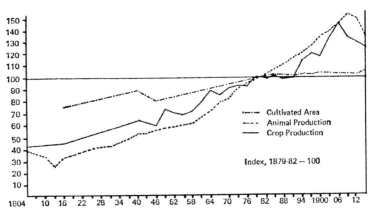

Source: K. Borchardt, "The Industrial Revolution in Germany 1700–1940," in *The Fontana Economic History of Europe*, ed. C. M. Cipolla, vol. 4.1 (London, 1973), 76–160, here 100.

2. Related thereto, the introduction of new crops, with higher output per hectare. Thus, root crops (potatoes and sugar-beets) went from 3 percent to 24 percent of total agricultural production between 1800 and 1843. Such crops were a large part of the crop-rotation system, and were grown on land that had previously been left fallow.[8] This growth continued over the second half of the century. By 1913 potatoes, for example, took up about one-seventh of the country's total supply of agricultural land.[9]

3. The diffusion of knowledge and improved technology among German farmers. Artificial fertilizers, the result of improved agricultural chemistry, helped improve productivity.

8. This is one reason why potatoes may have played a strategic role in Germany's development. Another is that they supplied Germany's growing numbers of agricultural workers with relatively inexpensive nutrition—quite likely an important factor sustaining the rising inputs of labor in agriculture in these years. K. Borchardt, "The Industrial Revolution in Germany 1700–1914," in *Fontana Economic History of Europe*, ed. C. M. Cipolla, vol. 4.1: *The Emergence of Industrial Societies* (London, 1973), 76–160.

9. Potatoes probably had their greatest impact in the first half of the century. See J. Komlos, "The New World's Contribution to Food Consumption during the Industrial Revolution," *Journal of European Economic History* 27 (1998): 67–82; also R. Dickler, "Organization and Change in Productivity in Eastern Prussia," in *European Peasants and Their Markets: Essays in Agrarian Change*, ed. W. N. Parker and E. Jones (Princeton, 1975), 269–92.

4. The mechanization of agricultural production. The rising wages of agricultural workers stimulated interest in reducing the cost of labor inputs, leading, eventually, to the introduction of family workers and, more importantly, machines, such as steam ploughs, reapers, cream separators, and so forth. This element clearly had its more important effects after 1850.
5. Taking output per man-year as a guide, the increased willingness of agricultural families to work longer hours, a phenomenon related to reforms that reduced the share of output payable in dues to others (non-family "stakeholders"), was probably an additional source of productivity increase in the 1850–1913 period.[10]

Some scholars, including Paul Bairoch, believe that the increase in agricultural productivity starting around 1850 may be considered a type of agricultural revolution paralleling industrial improvements.[11] In some cases, agricultural improvements came even earlier than industrial ones, and actually served as a precondition for the industrial revolution. They supplied industry with an abundant labor force, fed the new industrial workers, provided raw-materials (such as flax and wool) and contributed to a rise in demand for agricultural products. Without a doubt, there are important interrelations between agriculture and industry.[12]

However, it is hard to say whether causality goes in one, or in both directions. Agriculture may have fulfilled some necessary preconditions for industrialization, but some industrialization also took place entirely without agricultural improvements or before other improvements had been made. France, for example, may be a case showing how old-fashioned agricultural methods hindered industrial expansion.[13] Belgium, on the other hand, might be an example of industrialization caused entirely by export and

10. On this point, see M. Kopsidis, *Marktintegration und Entwicklung der westfälischen Landwirtschaft, 1780–1880. Marktorientierte ökonomische Entwicklung eines bäuerlich strukturierten Agrarsektors* (Münster, 1996), 31–40 and 242–43.

11. P. Bairoch, *The Economic Development of the Third World since 1900* (Berkeley, 1975), and idem, "Agriculture and the Industrial Revolution," in *Fontana Economic History of Europe*, ed. C. M. Cipolla, vol. 3 (London, 1969).

12. Cf. T. Pierenkemper, "Der Agrarsektor im Entwicklungsprozeß- Einige theoretische Vorüberlegungen," in *Landwirtschaft und industrielle Entwicklung. Zur ökonomischen Bedeutung von Bauernbefreiung, Agrarreform und Agrarrevolution*, ed. T. Pierenkemper (Stuttgart, 1989), 121–28.

13. See P. K. O'Brien and C. Keyder, *Economic Growth in Britain and France, 1780–1914* (London, 1978). In this book, the authors see agriculture as that sector in

import substitution, without any stimulus from improvements in domestic agriculture.

There is yet a third possibility, suggested some years ago by John Komlos as a general characteristic of nineteenth-century European industrialization: that agricultural improvements accompanying industrial expansion prevented—for the first time in modern history—the outbreak of the Malthusian crises that had inevitably followed previous waves of economic expansion.[14] In fact, in the case of Germany a kind of Malthusian crisis related to crop failures in agriculture did emerge in the 1840s, but by long-term historical standards it was mild in its effects and soon overcome. Moreover, a crisis of such proportions did not recur before 1914. We thus see here that crucial importance can be attached to what did not happen, in Sherlock Holmseian terms, to the importance of "the dog that didn't bark," in our case to the crisis that did not happen. Testing this hypothesis for the nineteenth century, however, really calls for evidence on its applicability to previous centuries as well; and that is beyond the scope of this book.

In the 1970s and 1980s, economic historians asked how German agriculture could have maintained its momentum in the face of new international competition from the U.S., South America, and Australia. Germany's competitors in these far off places were in fact aided by improvements in transportation technology (steamships, railroads) and by the superior character of their natural resources. In one sense, German agriculture responded appropriately to this international challenge: namely, by shifting away from grain and toward animal production (which by 1913 accounted for over two-thirds of the total value of German agricultural output).[15] This was only a partial retreat, however, and was weakened in its effects by protectionist interests. For in Germany, as in other European countries, protective tariffs became the dominant response, one that softened the impact of overseas competition. This helped German farmers, but, as in Europe today, such effects really came at the expense of German consumers. They are thus a topic deserving our further attention.

---

which French backwardness relative to Britain was most pronounced. Note the much greater relative size of the French agricultural sector, however.

14. J. Komlos, *Nutrition and Economic Development in the Eighteenth-Century Habsburg Monarchy: An Anthropometric History* (Princeton, 1989), esp. 198–205 and 219–23.

15. See the estimates in Hoffmann (1965), table 56.

Agricultural Protection

There has not been a great deal of English-language literature on German tariff policy. The interest of English and American scholars seems to have been directed more toward questions of social change in rural society rather than toward agriculture's economic problems. One important exception, however, is in the work of Steven B. Webb.[16] As his work shows, by 1879 Germany had definitely abandoned its free-trade policies. The newly introduced system of tariffs was designed to protect the economic interests of heavy industry (tariffs on iron) as well as of grain agriculture, and was both cause and effect of a powerful alliance of "iron and rye." This reflected the policies of Bismarck and of the Conservative Party. Agrarian interest groups, consisting largely of large estate owners, pressured Bismarck in favor of these policies, desiring protection for grain and sugar-beets. The peasantry specialized in animal husbandry also sought protection from foreign competition.

Tariffs were imposed on almost all imports except raw materials. Agricultural duties were the most important of these because

1. they became relatively high,
2. they had a direct impact on consumers,
3. most imports were agricultural products (or duty-free raw materials),
4. much of the labor force still worked in agriculture, and
5. they particularly benefited the Junkers—the large estate owners—who still dominated the political system.

Until about mid-century, Germany had been a major grain exporter (to England), but found itself undercut by new competitors such as the U.S., Russia, Australia, and South America which benefited from improved and cheaper railway and steamship transport. This foreign market was soon lost for German agricultural producers.

In light of German agriculture's increasing dependence on domestic markets, the government felt it had to act, or face the serious consequences of strong foreign pressure on the nation's agricultural sector, namely the concomitant political pressure on itself from alarmed farmers. It therefore imposed tariffs for both

16. S. B. Webb, "Agricultural Protection in Wilhelmine Germany: Forging an Empire with Pork and Rye," *Journal of Economic History* 42 (1982): 309–26.

economic and political reasons. Tariffs might also be said to have stabilized the political system of the German Empire, since they represented subsidies for the Junkers.

Some have wondered, without coming up with a satisfactory explanation, why peasants in the west supported the Junkers in the East. Hardach[17] argued that neither eastern estate owners nor western peasants benefited much from the tariffs, since the eastern and western markets were completely separate: In the East exports predominated and were dependent on international prices, whereas in the west, imports became more expensive for consumers. High transportation costs separated the eastern and western markets making it cheaper to ship grain from the U.S. to the Ruhr than from East Prussia. In fact, however, this holds true only for wheat production, on which Hardach's argument heavily concentrates, but not for rye production, which was the most important German export product. For this reason, Hardach's argument is somewhat misleading.

In contrast to Hardach, Alexander Gerschenkron[18] argued that tariffs had mixed results. Large landlords received the protection they wanted, while peasants suffered from it. Tariffs made fodder more expensive for peasants specialized in raising animals (especially hogs). Thus, landlords benefited from tariffs at the expense of peasants as well as consumers.

In 1902, however, Adolph Wagner[19] claimed that all branches of agriculture had benefited from the tariffs. According to his account, estate owners benefited from higher tariffs through the increased income they insured, while peasants received non-pecuniary gains, such as recognition of their demand for the protection of stockbreeding in the form of import regulations for hogs and frozen beef. This argument was taken up again by Steven Webb eighty years later and used as a part of his quantitative assessment of the tariffs.

Webb also took up crucial questions concerning *the protective effect of the tariffs of 1879* and its burden. One of these includes the extent to which German prices rose above world prices as a result. A look at statistics from the period preceding the tariffs shows that domestic prices in Eastern and Western Germany were more

17. G. Hardach, *Die Bedeutung wirtschaftlicher Faktoren bei der Wiedereinführung der Eisen- und Getreidezölle in Deutschland 1879* (Berlin, 1967).

18. A. Gerschenkron, *Bread and Democracy in Germany* (Berkeley, 1943).

19. Wagner (1901).

closely correlated between 1872 and 1879 than were prices between East Germany and the World Market. This means that we can reject Hardach's thesis that neither Junkers nor peasants benefited from the tariffs.

The following tables, taken from Webb's work, give an idea of the protective effects of the 1879 tariffs (and their successors). Note that the tables include estimates of "effective protection" (see table 21). This useful concept measures the relation of a tariff to the final price minus the tariff on imported inputs used to produce it, that is, on the value added, and not as in the usual tariff measure, in relation to the price of the protected product.

Tariffs for wheat and rye rose from about 10 marks per ton in 1879 to 30 in 1885 and 50 in 1887. This remarkable increase was partly checked in 1891–92 (falling to 35 marks per ton) because of lower wheat and rye prices. Nevertheless the margin of protection remained high.

Fodder grains experienced different forms of protection. Oats received protection at levels similar to wheat and rye, while barley duties were only half as high. Oats were produced mainly by large estates, while barley was used as fodder by smaller peasants in the south. Low prices helped to gain the support of southern peasants for the tariff policy. The tariffs initiated in 1879 raised the price of oats and rye somewhat above world market prices, causing a production increase in agriculture which far outstripped demand. For

Table 21: Tariff Protection for Arable Agriculture (1883–1913)

Product	1883–85	1889–90	1894–96	1900–1902	1906–8	1911–13
		Nominal Protection (percent)				
1. Rye	8	46	42	33	37	40
2. Wheat	6	33	32	27	36	33
3. Oats	9	34	31	25	42	39
4. Barley	4	17	20	17	10	10
5. Sugar (raw)	15	17	2	35	0	0
		Effective Protection (percent)				
6. Rye	9	49	46	37	42	48
7. Wheat	7	34	33	28	39	37
8. Oats	9	36	33	27	47	47
9. Barley	4	17	22	19	12	12

Source: S. B. Webb, "Agricultural Protection in Wilhelmine Germany: Forging an Empire with Pork and Rye," *Journal of Economic History* 42 (1982), 309–26, here 314.

this reason, the government offered a subsidy for grain exports in 1894. Starting in 1907–8, German exports even began to exceed imports. The period was marked by an enormous expansion of Germany's domestic agricultural production. In spite of the country's rapid industrialization and urbanization since 1870 Germany's economy remained largely self-sufficient in supplies of foodstuffs. Over this period the share of imports in domestic consumption of the four main cereals plus potatoes and meat (measured in money spent) changed as follows:

1870–72	5.2 percent
1889–91	15.5 percent
1910–12	9.3 percent

Since this measure excludes some products of growing significance which originated almost exclusively in Germany (such as dairy products, fresh fruit and vegetables, etc.), it is almost certainly an overestimate of the significance of imports. Interestingly enough, the greatest rates of productivity increase were realized by Germany's root crops, sugar beets, and potatoes. Sugar beets were an input into a mass product, sugar, while potatoes, besides being an important part of mass consumption, helped in the manufacture of alcohol. These were important parts of German agriculture. Potatoes, owing to their bulkiness, did not figure heavily in international trade, and thus attracted no tariff protection. Sugar beets, on the other hand, enjoyed heavy subsidies. Indeed, Germany became the world's largest producer of sugar in 1907, with 22 percent of global production. Its large exporters were subsidized in order to keep domestic prices of sugar above world-market prices, while imports were taxed. Export subsidies were largely financed by a sugar-production tax, which resulted in redistribution of income from farm producers to exporters. In our opinion, this was an absurdity, since it moved money from the producers' pockets to the merchants', completely bypassing consumers.

Agrarian protection had some interesting distributional implications. In effect arable agriculture received high protection, which amounted to a subsidy of the Junkers' most important crops. The less important crops i.e., those produced by the smaller-scale peasant farmers, enjoyed less protection. These smaller producers, for example, tended to rely more on livestock and animal production; and pork, beef and milk therefore made up much of their business. They also benefited from non-tariff restrictions (health-regulations, for example) which thus protected German animals from

diseases, consumers from inferior meat, and farmers from competition, reflected, for instance, in the stop of live hog imports in the
mid 1890s. Such protection came their way, politically speaking, in
order to hold them—and their considerable voting power—in the
"protectionist camp."

Owing to space limitations it is not possible to consider even
some of the most important details of this protectionist development, e.g., the fact that live-pork imports subsequently increased
for a while, or that milk production benefited from tariffs on butter
and cheese, but egg production did not. Nevertheless, a relevant
picture of the general development is given in table 22. The figures
there, when compared with those of our table 21, help make a good
case for the argument that the larger-scale producers benefited most.

Of course, this does not entirely resolve the important question
of the distribution of the protective system's benefits. Following
Webb's analysis, however, we draw on the 1907 agricultural census and compute the share of protected products for different sizes
of farms (see table 23).

Table 22: Tariff Protection for Animal Husbandry (1883–1913)

Product	1883–85	1889–90	1894–96	1900–1902	1906–8	1911–13
	Nominal Protection (percent)					
1. Live hogs	3	7	6	6	8	7
2. Fresh pork	–	–	–	16	29	26
3. Live cattle	2	3	3	3	7	9
4. Frozen beef	–	–	–	11	26	32
5. Butter	14	14	14	12	10	9
6. Cheese, soft	13	14	15	15	12	12
7. Cheese, hard	13	14	11	11	11	10
8. Milk	16	14	15	13	11	9
9. Eggs	3	3	3	3	3	3
10. Ave. traded folder	6	21	15	19	19	19
	Effective Protection (percent)					
11. Live hogs	2	4	4	–	–	–
12. Fresh hogs	–	–	–	16	31	27
13. Live cattle	0	-4	-3	–	–	–
14. Frozen beef	–	–	–	10	28	36
15. Milk	19	12	13	12	9	6
16. Eggs	2	-3	-3	-1	-2	-2

Source: Webb (1982), 319.

Table 23: Shares of Value Added by Major Products in Each Farm Category

Product	Size (hectares)					
	0–2	2–5	5–10	10–20	20–100	over 100
Rye	.06	.11	.10	.12	.13	.14
Wheat	.01	.03	.03	.05	.05	.08
Oats	.03	.07	.08	.10	.11	.12
Barley	.02	.03	.03	.04	.04	.05
Sugar	.01	.02	.02	.02	.04	.14
Potatoes	.19	.13	.09	.09	.07	.13
Pork	.38	.18	.16	.17	.13	.08
Beef	.05	.11	.16	.20	.17	.14
Milk	.25	.32	.31	.23	.25	.11

Source: Webb (1982), 324.

Using 1907 as a base year, we can calculate the average amount of protection given to various sizes of farms at various times. The results are in table 24. They document rising protectionism, at first largely for the benefit of the large-scale grain producers. From the 1890s on, however, the smaller-scale producers caught up.

It was the consumer who had to pay for this protection. In 1907, probably about 1 percent of German GNP was redistributed in this way from urban workers to rural estates and from the peasantry to grain growers. Domestic prices remained continually above international levels. In addition, about 2 percent of GNP went toward subsidization of cattle and hog farmers. All told, this redistribution of wealth thus amounted to around 3 percent of the country's GNP; it did not make many German farmers wealthy, but it did slow the pace of the agricultural sector's adaptation of the agricultural sector, a negative development for an industrializing nation. This process lasted well into the twentieth century.

Table 24: Average Effective Protection for Various Farm-Size Categories (in percent)

Size Category	1883–85	1889–90	1893–95	1900–1902	1906–8	1911–13
0–2 hectares	7	9	9	14	20	19
2–5 hectares	9	14	14	16	21	21
5–10 hectares	9	14	14	16	22	23
10–20 hectares	7	15	14	17	25	26
20–100 hectares	9	17	16	19	24	25
Over 100 hectares	8	19	16	22	23	24

Source: Webb (1982), 325.

Chapter Six

POPULATION AND LABOR

Population and Migration

The expansion of Germany's agricultural production, described in the previous chapter, was closely related to the country's population growth. More agricultural output meant more nutrients and hence, a better-fed population. On the other hand, more agricultural production also meant, all things remaining equal, a greater demand for labor, positive incentives for having more children, and thus population growth. Observing that every child has two hands with which to work and a mouth with which to eat, we can argue that the economic value of each new child should be reflected in the balance of its potential additions to production and consumption. It is then only a small step to speculate that family decisions about having children should tend to reflect, historically, expectations about that potential: the greater the expected surplus of production over consumption, the more likely that more children will be born. This line of reasoning, oversimplified and one-sided as it is, takes us into the field of demography, the study of population change. In this chapter we wish to draw on concepts from the field of demography in order to describe the changes that took place in Germany's population in the nineteenth century and to discuss some of their probable causes.

Population Growth

The quantitative record of Germany's population before 1800 is extremely spotty. We have reason to believe that population was

growing over most of the eighteenth century, but that it was subject to severe shocks from time to time, related to crop failures,
wars, or to both killers simultaneously. These shocks led to upward surges in death rates and declines in birth rates, the latter in
part resulting from local populations adjusting to reduced economic opportunities by marrying later or not at all. This seems to
have happened around 1739–40, when the supply of food fell in
some places by 20 to 30 percent, again in 1755–56, and then again
in the early 1770s, when a crop failure affected not only much of
Germany but most of Europe as well.[1] Nevertheless, the dominant tendency from the 1770s on was an excess of births over
deaths, i.e., population growth.

In the nineteenth century, population growth continued and in
all probability accelerated. Within the German boundaries of 1871,
the German population grew from 24 to nearly 30 million between
1800 and 1830, a change that translates into an annual growth rate
of about 0.7 percent. One of the more remarkable episodes of this
period was the post-Napoleonic "baby boom" (c. 1816–25), which
was marked by growth rates double their long-run level and which
may have had lasting effects on the German demographic structure.[2] Be that as it may, over the rest of the century growth continued, slowing down briefly during the crisis of the 1840s and then

Table 25: Varying Views on Population Increase from 1800 to 1830 in Germany,
Borders of 1871 (in millions)

	Fischer	Hoffmann	Wehler	Dipper	Growth Rate (%)
1800	–	–	24.5	23.0	
					0.63
1810	–	–	25.5	24.4	
					0.16
1815	23.7	25.0	–	24.6	
	(1817)	(1817)			1.38
1820	–	26.1	26.3	26.3	
					1.03
1830	28.2	29.4	29.5	29.5	
	(1831)				

Source: C. Dipper, *Deutsche Geschichte 1648–1789* (Frankfurt am Main, 1991), 73.

1. On this "pre-industrial" experience, see W. Abel, *Massenarmut und Hungerkrisen im vorindustriellen Europa*, 2nd ed. (Göttingen, 1977).
2. See on this W. R. Lee, "Germany," in *European Demography and Economic
Growth*, ed. W. R. Lee (London, 1979), 144–95.

again in the 1880s, but accelerating once more from the 1890s to World War I.

Tables 25 and 26 and graph 10 here illustrate the overall temporal pattern. In table 26 and graph 10 we see that natural increase, i.e., the surplus of births over deaths, caused this growth. Note also, however, that emigration remained significant until the 1890s. Up to then it thus worked as a brake on growth. This was a positive

Table 26: Population Growth in Germany (1816–1980) (in 1,000s and rates per 1,000 inhabitants)

Year	Population (in thousands)	Annual Growth (0/00)	Annual Natural Increase (0/00)	Annual Net Migration (0/00)
1816*	23,520			
1841*	31,480	11.7	12.0	-0.4
1871	40,995	8.8	8.2	+0.6**
1900	56,046	10.8	12.6	-1.9
1925	62,411	4.3	9.1	-4.7**
1943	70,411	6.5	6.0	+0.6

*Territory of the German Reich. **Comprises territorial change.

Source: P. Marschalck, *Bevölkerungsgeschichte Deutschlands im 19. und 20. Jahrhundert* (Frankfurt am Main, 1981), 145–47.

Graph 10: Natural Population Movement in Germany (1816–1980)

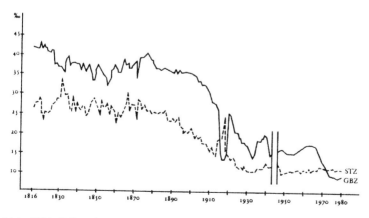

Note: 1816–40 Prussia, 1841–1943 German Reich, 1946–80 Federal Republic of Germany

Source: Marschalck (1984), 183.

development, representing a lowering of the pressure of population on relatively scarce resources (recall the remarks about overpopulation and labor surplus in chapter 3). And it was the deepening of industrialization in Germany at the end of the nineteenth century that turned the chronic outflow of migrants into an inflow. We shall return to this point below.

Population Dynamics

In order to answer the crucial question—why did the German population grow in the nineteenth century?—we need to look more closely at its dynamics. Population growth is the outcome of an interplay of births, deaths and migration. The difference between births and deaths is called "natural increase." A long-established demographic convention defines birth rates as the number of births per year per 1,000 inhabitants and death rates as the number of deaths per year and 1,000 inhabitants. Migration rates are similarly defined, though in practice migration measurement has proved to be difficult.[3] We look first at the pattern of birth and death rates.

We begin the discussion of this pattern by drawing on a taxonomic device which has been widely used by demographers and demographic historians and summarized as the "Demographic Transition Theory" (DTT). The DTT purports to depict certain stylized facts about population change which are believed to mark the demographic history of virtually countries. Graph 11 offers a capsule view of the DTT.

Graph 11 corresponds roughly to the following development pattern:

Stage 1: A pre-industrial demographic regime, which refers to high fertility, high mortality, causing no dramatic growth in population.

Stage 2: Declining mortality and high fertility causes increased and sustained population growth.

Stage 3: Declining mortality but less swiftly declining fertility results in declining population growth, but still increasing total population.

---

3. In fact, over long stretches of the nineteenth century, net migration—the magnitude we are most interested in here—has frequently been measured as the residual of the difference between observed population change and the estimated natural increase. See W. Köllmann, *Bevölkerung in der Industriellen Revolution* (Göttingen, 1974).

Graph 11: Principles of Demographic Transition

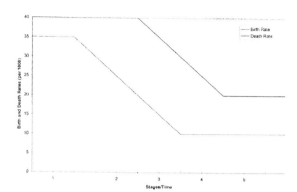

Source: Adapted from A. E. Imhof, *Einführung in die historische Demographie* (Munich, 1977), 61.

Stage 4: Low mortality and declining fertility leads to moderate population growth.

Stage 5: Low mortality and low fertility results in no dramatic growth in population, which is the industrial demographic regime.

The DTT raises three very important questions related to Germany's demographic history. First, why did mortality rates fall in Stage 2? The question has received two competing answers. The first one stresses the increased and more stable supply of foodstuffs which came about, particularly after 1850, as agricultural production increased and the spreading railroad network lowered food distribution costs. This is felt to have increased the population's resistance to disease. The second answer focuses attention on improved medical technology and especially improved public health conditions, e.g., water supply, sanitation, etc., which lowered the incidence of diseases, especially contagious ones. Readers should be warned here, however, that the change in the overall death rate may give a too optimistic picture of nineteenth-century progress. If one takes infant mortality as a guide, thus focusing on a constant age group (from 0 to 1), one will find no significant improvement until after around 1900. Table 27 shows this result.[4]

4. See R. Spree, *Soziale Ungleichheit vor Krankheit und Tod* (Göttingen, 1981).

Table 27: Life Expectancy and Infant Mortality in Germany (eighteenth to twentieth century)

	Year	Life expectancy at birth yearly	Infant deaths per 1,000 live births
	1700*	30.0	
	1750*	32.5	300.0–500.0
	1850*	35.0	
	1871–80	37.0	235.0
	1891–1900	42.3	216.0
	1932–34	61.3	85.0**
FRG	1949–51	66.5	55.1
	1978–80	73.0	13.5
GDR	1952	65.9	72.2***
	1979	71.7	12.9

*Estimates. **1930. ***1950.

Source: P. Marschalck (1984), 164–68.

Second, why did birth rates stay high in Stage 2 after death rates had begun to fall significantly? Why this lag? Once again, the field of historical demography has two answers ready for us. The first of these simply contends that there is no lag. For if one corrects for the changing age structure of the population—and it should be readily apparent that the relative number of women in child-bearing age will have an important effect on the overall birth rate of a population—and takes measured fertility, rather than crude birth rates, as the relevant index, then the discrepancy in timing disappears, because fertility clearly falls from the 1870s on. This finding has not been accepted by all historians, however.[5] Many of these scholars emphasize a second putative cause: the widening of employment opportunities in Germany since the 1850s, which would have increased family demand for children, either because rising incomes related to higher employment made an increase in family size easier, or because those opportunities included child labor. Köllmann, a demographic historian, compared the pre-1850 and post-1850 periods and found a significant rise in jobs relative to those seeking work after 1850.[6] That pattern fits the argument.

5. Knodel's serious analysis really begins around 1870, so there is room for doubt about the behavior of fertility before then. See J. Knodel, *The Decline of Fertility in Germany, 1871–1939* (Princeton, 1976).
6. See W. Köllmann, "Bevölkerung und Arbeitskräftepotential in Deutschland, 1815–1870," reprinted in idem, *Bevölkerung in der industriellen Revolution* (Göttingen, 1974).

Graph 12: Demographic Indices (1867–1961)

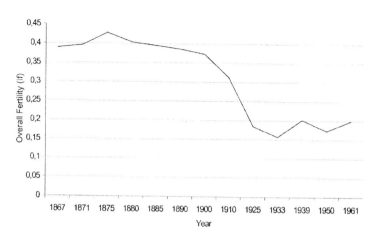

Source: Data from J. Knodel, *The Decline of Fertility in Germany, 1871–1939* (Princeton, 1976).

The third important question related to DTT follows: Why did birth rates fall so dramatically in Stage 3? Here we find a greater consensus, though there are differences of opinion concerning the weighting. The preferred answer is that the demand for children declined significantly from the 1870s on. For one thing, urbanization, which accelerated after 1870 and affected an ever-growing share of the total population, was characterized by high and rising child-raising costs, e.g., related to housing, and this will have inhibited family size. For another, Bismarck's celebrated social insurance program, initiated in the 1880s, began to diminish the need for children to provide old-age security for their parents. And finally, it may be that the costs of family limitation, of family planning, began to fall at the end of the century, thus enabling families to better realize the aim of a smaller family than had earlier been the case. Some evidence points in this direction.[7]

This book cannot discuss the validity or accuracy of these answers. Nor can it attempt to weight their relative merits. Readers will have to accept them as plausible hypotheses about Germany's nineteenth-century demographic transition. They should bear in

7. See J. Knodel, *Demographic Behavior in the Past* (Cambridge, 1988), where this evidence is discussed.

mind, however, that this transition, especially Stage 3, is one of the most universal characteristics of the economic modernization of nations. Germany's nineteenth-century experience is by no means abnormal or unusual. The DTT approach, however, builds on aggregate data on birth and death rates. One drawback is that the data used to illustrate it conceal some interesting details. In regions with higher industrial growth rates, such as Prussia and Saxony, increases in population growth rates started earlier, widening differences between the birth and mortality lines in the graph. In agricultural regions, the same process was hampered and delayed. Therefore, aggregate German development does not adequately reflect the ongoing changes in the country, especially on a regional level.

In fact, regional differences such as these might help us to better understand why birth and death rates fell when they did. A second deficiency is that the DTT does not do justice to the important role played by migration. Migration is important enough to deserve more attention. It therefore forms the subject of the following subsection.

Migration

As we saw earlier, migration has been an important factor in Germany's population history. In the nineteenth century, migration was, among other things, an economic mechanism that responded to discrepancies between labor demand and labor supply. This was true of internal migration (between the different regions of Germany) as well as of international migration. The most dramatic movements involved overseas migration, with which our description therefore begins.

Transnational migration was dominated by the transatlantic migration to North America. It began long before the nineteenth century, to be exact, on 9 October 1683, when thirteen Mennonite families from Krefeld landed in Philadelphia. Many other religious groups of migrants would follow their example. The nineteenth century was the true era of mass migration, however, and its basis was largely economic. By that we mean that it largely reflected an oversupply of labor in relation to employment opportunities. It took manifold forms. Until the 1860s most of the German emigrants came from the southern states of Germany (Palatinate, Württemberg, Baden) and traveled northwards up the Rhine to the ports of embarkation. These were regions in which equal inheritance laws and small-plot agriculture prevailed. The high post-1815 rates of natural increase (see table 25) put pressure on this system and threatened to create what one observer called "dwarf agriculture" (consisting of inefficiently small farms). In economic terms, the supply of land and capital was inadequate to provide productive employment for additional labor, and migration was a means of getting rid of the surplus.

Roughly the same argument applies to a second major source of German emigration, one which has often been overlooked. This is the emigration from regions, especially in northern Germany, in which rural industry (or proto-industry) connected with the domestic manufacture of linens, played an important role. These proto-industrial centers faced, since the 1820s, severe competition from the mechanized factory production of linens and cottons in Great Britain as well as in Germany itself. Such regions, found in western Hanover, in East Westphalia and in western parts of Münsterland on the Dutch border, were hosts, so to speak, to "dying industries" and increasing numbers of underemployed workers.[8] In addition, there is evidence of a general oversupply of artisans and craft workers in many parts of Germany, indicated, e.g., by the shrinking number of artisans per producing unit, which lasted well into the 1850s.[9] Finally, from the 1860s on, East Elbian Prussia became the principal source of German emigration, as its agriculture, facing increasingly strong competition from overseas grain producers, proved no longer able or willing to absorb the labor surpluses there.[10]

We have been describing the economic conditions which promoted emigration from Germany. These are often called "push" factors, and may be distinguished from the "pull" factors, meaning the conditions that attached migrants to the target country. It will come as no surprise to learn that over most of the nineteenth century, employment opportunities in the U.S. were much greater and wage levels higher than in Germany. This economic gap worked so to speak as a constant attractive force. Emigration from Germany to the U.S., however, took place in waves. It seems that conditions

8. See on this the valuable work of W. Kamphoefner, *The Westfalians: From Germany to Missouri* (Princeton, 1987).
9. See once again Köllmann (1974), 61–98.
10. Here R. A. Dickler, "Organization and Change in Productivity in Eastern Prussia. Labor Market Pressure Aspects of Agricultural Growth in the Eastern Region of Prussia, 1840–1914: A Case Study of Economic Demographic Transition" (Ph.D. diss., University of Pennsylvania, 1975).

had to deteriorate dramatically in Germany or radically improve in the U.S. to set off a transatlantic movement. Our table 28 and graph 13 show the temporal pattern. Poor conditions in Germany conditioned the movements of 1816–19 (harvest failures) and especially the late 1840s and early 1850s (a delayed response to the crisis of 1845–47), but from the 1850s on, improving employment opportunities in the U.S. played a more significant role.

If we are interested in the cause of transatlantic migration, we also need to think about a factor of secularly increasing importance:

Graph 13: Phases of German Transatlantic Migration (1830–1932)

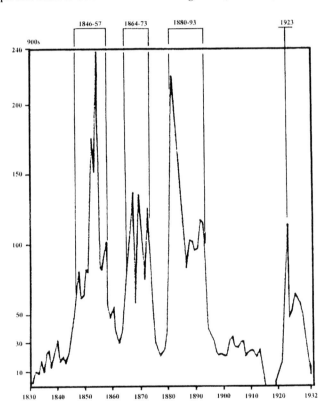

Source: K. J. Bade, "Die deutsche überseeische Massenauswanderung im 19. und frühen 20. Jahrhundert. Bestimmungsfaktoren und Entwicklungsbedingungen," in idem, *Auswanderer-Wanderarbeiter-Gastarbeiter. Bevölkerung, Arbeitsmarkt und Wanderung in Deutschland in der Mitte des 19. Jahrhunderts*, vol. 1 (2 vols.) (Ostfildern, 1984), 259–99, here 264.

Table 28: German Emigration (1816–1914)

Year	Emigration (1,000s)	Year	Emigration (1,000s)	Year	Emigration (1,000s)
1816–1819	25.0	1855	83.8	1890	97.1
–	–	1856	80.9	1891	120.1
1820	3.0	1857	103.1	1892	116.3
1821	2.8	1858	56.8	1893	87.7
1822	1.1	1859	47.4	1894	41.0
1823	1.3	–	–	–	–
1824	1.6	1860	57.9	1895	37.5
–	–	1861	36.1	1896	33.8
1825	3.2	1862	31.4	1897	24.6
1826	1.4	1863	39.0	1898	22.2
1827	1.2	1864	60.7	1899	24.3
1828	5.2	–	–	–	–
1829	1.7	1865	88.7	1900	22.3
–	–	1866	120.4	1901	22.1
1830	5.5	1867	138.4	1902	32.1
1831	7.2	1868	59.0	1903	36.3
1832	11.2	1869	136.2	1904	28.0
1833	7.7	–	–	–	–
1834	19.5	1870	122.2	1905	28.1
–	–	1871	76.2	1906	31.1
1835	9.1	1872	128.2	1907	31.7
1836	22.8	1873	110.4	1908	19.9
1837	26.1	1874	47.6	1909	24.9
1838	12.9	–	–	–	–
1839	23.1	1875	32.3	1910	25.5
–	–	1876	26.6	1911	22.7
1840	32.7	1877	22.9	1912	18.5
1841	16.8	1879	35.9	1914	11.8
1842	22.4	1879	35.9	1914	11.8
1843	15.9	–	–	–	–
1844	22.9	1880	117.1	–	–
–	–	1881	220.9	–	–
1845	37.8	1882	203.6	–	–
1846	63.3	1883	173.6	–	–
1847	80.3	1884	149.1	–	–
1848	62.8	–	–	–	–
1849	64.2	1885	110.1	–	–
–	–	1886	83.2	–	–
1850	83.2	1887	104.8	–	–
1851	78.8	1888	104.0	–	–
1852	176.4	1889	96.1	–	–
1853	150.7	–	–	–	–
1854	239.2	–	–	–	–

Source: P. Marschalck, *Deutsche Überseewanderungen im 19. Jahrhundert. Ein Beitrag zur soziologischen Theorie der Bevölkerung* (Stuttgart, 1973), 35–37.

immigration as a motor behind the creation of a new market for shipping services. The eastward bound shipments of raw cotton had long "cried for" a westward bound ballast that European emigrants now supplied. Their needs stimulated capacity increases, and these, in turn, stimulated emigration from German port cities. As one can imagine, these port cities such as Hamburg and Bremen competed for lucrative transportation to America; shipping lines did excellent business; and newspaper advertisers for the transportation industry, agents, writers, and insurance companies got a piece of the pie, too. The same was true when German emigration to the U.S. reached its second peak, between 1866 and 1873, following the depression of the late 1850s. The American Civil War interrupted immigration to the U.S., so there was a backlog of emigrants waiting to re-enter the U.S. at the end of the conflict.

Transatlantic migration slowed down dramatically in the 1890s, as the great boom of the German economy of these years generated stronger labor demands, larger wage increases, and slowed German emigration.[11] Indeed, Germany became a magnet for immigrant workers, from Italy, Czarist Poland, and elsewhere. This is worth a brief discussion.

One of the more interesting episodes in late-nineteenth-century German immigration concerns the East Elbian agricultural labor market. The mass exodus of German agricultural workers from East Elbia in the 1880s led to severe seasonal shortages of labor there. The answer of the East Elbian estate owners—aided by German government officials—lay in the recruitment of cheap labor from Czarist Russia's Poland and from the Ukraine. By the end of the nineteenth century, continental European labor immigration to Germany reached enormous proportions.[12] By 1913, there were almost one million seasonal agrarian workers in Germany. Graph 14 shows two ways to count seasonal workers. One curve shows seasonal workers counted at the end of the peak season, while the other shows the number of workers counted at the end of a calendar year. The sum of the two categories, farm and industrial laborers, gives us a total. The graph shows that regular year-round farm workers by no means dominated the overall equation, for they

11. On this, see J. G. Williamson, "The Evolution of Global Markets since 1830: Background Evidence and Hypotheses," *Economic History Review* 32 (1995): 141–96, esp. 153–57, where Europe as a whole as well as Latin America are discussed.

12. K. J. Bade, "Labor Migration and the State: Germany from the Late 19th Century to the Onset of the Great Depression," in *Population, Labor and Migration in 19th- and 20th-Century Germany*, ed. K.J. Bade (Leamington Spa, 1987), 59–85.

Graph 14: Foreign Labor in Prussia (1906–1914) (as registered by the Prussian Department of the Interior)

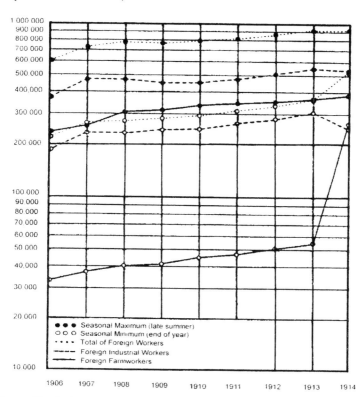

Source: K. J. Bade, "Labour Migration and the State: Germany from the Late 19th Century to the Onset of the Great Depression," in *Population, Labour and Migration in 19th- and 20th-Century Germany*, ed. K. J. Bade (Leamington Spa, 1987), 59–85, here 64.

numbered only between 200,000 and 400,000. Most of the foreign workers in Germany, however, were seasonal farm laborers. The total number of foreign workers in Prussia alone was one million, and the total was considerably higher for all of Germany.

This mass movement caused structural and political problems, since Russians and Poles, who formed the bulk of the foreign workers, were seen by the state of Prussia as security risks. We must not forget that the territory of the former Polish State was divided at the time between Russia, which had created a puppet Polish "kingdom," the Austro-Hungarian Empire, and

Graph 15: Foreign Workers by Countries of Origin in Prussia (1906–1914)

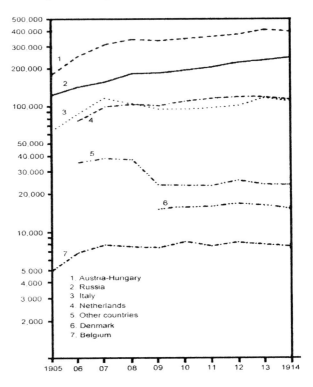

Source: Bade (1987), 67.

Prussian Germany. Germany now feared a "Polonization" of its eastern provinces, where a large Polish minority already lived. Therefore, the Prussian State resorted to a policy of Germanization for its Polish-speaking citizens, so as to prevent an influx of Polish nationalism.

A restrictive system was also implemented for Polish workers coming from the regions occupied by Russia. They were required to leave Germany before 20 December each year, and were not allowed to re-enter Germany before 1 February the following year. Such a policy made many Poles feel the widespread anti-Polish sentiment in Germany. Poles of non-German citizenship made up 71.5 percent of foreign farm workers in Prussia in 1906, but only 66.1 percent in 1913. Thus, we can speak about an "importation" of Polish labor, but not about true immigration.

Migration within Germany also responded to "push" and "pull" factors. To some extent, the same specific "push" factors that were operative in overseas migration also applied to internal migration. Regions with agricultural surplus labor and with dying proto-industries provided a disproportional share of emigrants. For most of the century, however, internal migration was largely short-range and seasonal. The timing was determined by the pull of demand in the industrializing centers. This remained typical until 1914. It is true, however, that a longer-range and more permanent type of internal migration set in during the 1890s, as German urbanization speeded up. The most dramatic example was the flow of workers from East Elbia to the Rhenish-Westphalian industrial cities, especially the Ruhr. For obvious reasons, the particular history of Polish immigration has been well studied. Table 29 offers an insight into this connection as well as its link to overseas migration. Note the relative concentration of Poles in areas outside, but near the major cities. More details need not be reported here, for the story of the East-West movement has been well told elsewhere.[13]

Labor Force Development

Population growth and migration in Germany after 1850 had a significant impact on the growth of the domestic labor force. In surveying this impact it is useful to distinguish between four different effects and fields of analysis:

1. a quantitative effect, related to the size and the structure of the labor force;
2. a qualitative effect, concerning the changing quality of the labor force;
3. living conditions (wages and income, work hours, and working conditions); and
4. an institutional effect, including unionization, the formation of trade associations, state regulations, and so forth.

13. W. Brepohl, *Der Aufbau des Ruhrvolks im Zuge der Ost-West-Wanderung. Beiträge zur deutschen Sozialgeschichte des 19. und 20. Jahrhunderts,* Soziale Forschung und Praxis 7 (Recklinghausen, 1948); Wolfgang Köllmann, "Industrialisierung, Binnenwanderung und 'soziale Frage,'" reprinted in idem, *Bevölkerung in der industriellen Revolution* (Göttingen, 1974), 106–24.

Table 29: Distribution of Polish Groups in the Areas of the Ruhr Containing the Highest Numbers of Poles (excluding Masurians and bilinguals)

Proportion of the Total Population	1890 Absolute	%	1900 Absolute	%	1905 Absolute	%	1910 absolute	%
Provincial government district of Münster								
Recklinghausen (Stadt)	716	5.1	6,389	18.8	9,250	20.8	12,404	23.1
Recklinghausen (Land)	3,988	5.8	15,495	12.3	23,777	13.3	40,847	15.7
Buer	553	5.0	4,115	14.4	4,895	12.2	7,259	11.8
Provincial government district of Arnsberg								
Hamm (Stadt)	11	0.04	66	0.2	145	0.4	198	0.5
Hamm (Land)	183	0.3	737	1.0	1,005	1.2	1,982	2.0
Dortmund (Stadt)	626	0.7	3,803	2.7	5,701	3.2	9,722	4.5
Dortmund (Land)	1,699	2.2	10,787	7.3	18,423	10.2	26,024	12.2
Hörde (Stadt)	177	1.1	703	2.8	1,052	3.7	1,466	4.5
Hörde (Land)	338	0.5	1,355	1.5	1,571	1.6	2,268	2.1
Bochum (Stadt)	1,120	2.4	1,841	2.8	4,673	3.9	6,269	4.6
Bochum (Land)	2,038	2.7	11,095	8.4	13,054	11.3	10,834	9.0
Witten	195	0.7	1,098	3.3	1,253	3.5	1,693	4.5
Herne	2,121	15.2	3,452	12.4	4,521	13.6	12,364	21.6
Gelsenkirchen (Stadt)	1,930	6.9	1,880	5.1	13,889	9.4	15,065	8.9
Gelsenkirchen (Land)	7,064	7.1	24,542	13.1	16,923	14.1	25,383	17.7
Hattingen	492	0.8	1,784	2.2	2,418	2.7	3,238	3.3
Provincial government district of Düsseldorf								
Duisburg	74	0.1	484	0.5	4,224	2.2	7,199	3.1
Oberhausen	668	2.6	2,743	6.5	4,898	9.4	8,641	9.6
Mülheim	12	0.04	176	0.5	1,276	1.4	2,089	1.9
Hamborn	27	0.6	3,055	9.4	10,493	15.6	17,432	17.1
Dinslaken	242	0.3	1,188	1.6	1,304	2.1	2,288	2.9
Essen (Stadt)	211	0.3	1,657	1.4	2,601	1.1	3,805	1.3
Essen (Land)	1,887	1.2	9,049	3.2	12,035	4.9	17,699	6.4

Source: C. Klessmann, "Long-Distance Migration. Integration and Segregation of an Ethnic Minority in Industrial Germany: The Case of the Ruhr Poles," in *Population, Labor and Migration in 19th- and 20th-Century Germany,* German Historical Perspectives 1, ed. K. J. Bade (Leamington Spa i.a., 1987), 101–14, here 105.

Size and Structure

The size and structure of the German labor force was a function of demographic expansion and of the distribution of workers by sex, age, skills, and occupation.[14] In 1816, for example, Germany (within the borders of 1871) had 23.5 million inhabitants, 10 million of whom made up the "labor force." In 1850, the figures were 35 and 15 million respectively, and by 1913 the population had grown to 67 million, of whom 27 million were "active" participants in the labor market. In other words, the work force almost tripled in a century. The participation rate remained stable at slightly over 40 percent during most of the century, though it increased to 51.3 percent by 1925 after World War I. Of course, the average varied for males and females with nearly three men for every one working woman in the pre-1914 period. Such rates meant that male participation in the economy was very high, especially if we exclude children and the elderly.[15]

Unfortunately, we cannot explain how these participation rates came about with any precision. A comparison of population growth of about 45 percent with labor force growth of close to 60 percent, between 1882 and 1913, means—in an accounting sense—that the former accounted for about 75 percent of the latter. In truth, however, population behavior and reproduction patterns affected labor with a lag of fifteen to twenty years. It is thus somewhat foolhardy to attempt to "explain" the participation rates with population alone. Different age groups, for example, had different participation rates, and those also differed along gender lines, resulting in different life-cycle employment patterns for men and women. Our tables 30 and 31 offer some rough quantitative measures of these changes.

Data on the sectoral distribution of the labor force show that agriculture lost its dominant position in the second half of the nineteenth century, falling from 55 percent to 34 percent of the total labor force by 1907. Over the same period, industry and services increased their shares to 40 percent and 26 percent respectively. Table 32, which divides the labor force into primary, secondary and tertiary sectors, documents these shifts. In industry (= secondary sector) and services (= the tertiary sector) technological and marketing improvements were partly responsible for the

---

14. Pierenkemper (1987).
15. J. J. Lee, "Labor in German Industrialization," in *Cambridge Economic History of Europe*, ed. Peter Mathias and M. M. Postan, vol. 7 (8 vols.) (Cambridge, 1978), 442–91.

Table 30: Employment Rate for the German Population (1882–1980)

Year	Share of the employed as percent of total population	Year	Share of the employed as percent of total population
1882	42.3	1939	50.8
1885	42.9	1950	47.0
1907	45.6	1961	46.1
1925	51.2	1967	44.5
1933	49.4	1980	42.8

Source: T. Pierenkemper, "The Standard of Living and Employment in Germany 1850–1980: An Overview," *Journal of European Economic History* 16 (1987): 51–73, here 57.

Table 31: Participation Rates (in percent)

Year	Both Sexes total	excluding relatives assisting	Male total	excluding relatives assisting	Female total	excluding relatives assisting
1882	41.6	37.5	60.5	56.1	23.5	19.6
1895	42.4	38.7	60.1	57.6	24.3	20.5
1907	45.2	38.2	61.9	57.4	29.7	19.6
(1907)*	(45.7)	(38.9)	(61.4)	(57.8)	(30.5)	(20.5)
1925	51.3	42.6	68.0	63.7	35.6	22.8

*Figures in parentheses for 1907 are for Germany within the borders of 1925.

Source: J. J. Lee, "Labor in German Industrialization," in *Cambridge Economic History of Europe*, ed. Peter Mathias and M. M. Postan, vol. 7.1 (8 vols.) (Cambridge, 1978), 442–91, here 444.

Table 32: Sectoral Distribution of the Labor Force (in percent)

	Primary	Secondary	Tertiary
1852	55	25	20
1880	49	30	21
1910	36	37	27

Source: Lee (1978), 445.

employment gains registered. Equally important were some shifts not recorded in table 32, e.g., the secularly growing number of white collar-employees, or the decline in the number of self-employed workers.

Quality of Labor

These quantitative shifts were accompanied by qualitative changes. Many contemporary economists argue that most economic growth is due to growth in the "quality of labor" rather than to investment in physical capital. Of course, "quality of labor" is hard to define, and evidence of a change in the quality of labor in Germany or anywhere else is difficult to produce. The skill and educational levels of the labor force certainly rose in the 1850–1914 period. Indeed, there is reason to see this improvement as one of the main sources of nineteenth-century economic growth.[16] Good data on this point, however, are not easy to find; for Germany, they are only readily available for 1933 (see table 33).[17] Figures for that year show that skilled workers made up 48.6 percent of the male labor force, semi-skilled workers made up 21.3 percent, and unskilled workers 30.1 percent. In the larger sectors, the ratio of skilled to non-skilled workers was even higher. In mechanical engineering, for example, 64 percent of the 233,000 employees were skilled. We may presume that such branch differences also characterized the pre-1914 period, since a number of studies point in this direction.[18]

How did a worker acquire a specific skill? In the early stages of industrialization, many skills and much knowledge had to be imported, along with raw materials and technology. Nonetheless, as we have seen in the example of the iron industry, a process of *import substitution* soon began which was to establish the superiority of domestic resources over foreign inputs.[19]

---

16. On this, see C. Buchheim, *Industrielle Revolutionen. Langfristige Entwicklung in Großbritannien, Europa und Übersee* (Munich, 1994), 149.

17. See Lee (1978), 447.

18. On this, see J. Kocka, *Unternehmensverwaltung und Angestelltenschaft am Beispiel Siemens, 1847–1914* (Stuttgart, 1969); H. von Laer, *Industrialisierung und Qualität der Arbeit. Eine bildungsökonomische Untersuchung für das 19. Jahrhundert* (New York, 1977); T. Pierenkemper, *Arbeitsmarkt und Angestellte im deutschen Kaiserreich, 1880–1913. Interessen und Strategien als Elemente der Integration eines segmentierten Arbeitsmarktes* (Stuttgart, 1987).

19. See R. Fremdling, "Der Puddler. Zur Sozialgeschichte eines Industriehandwerkers, in *Handwerkerschaft und Industrialisierung in Deutschland,* ed. U. Engelhardt

Table 33: Skill Distribution of Male Work Force (1933)

	Skilled		Semi-skilled		Others	
	1,000s	%	1,000s	%	1,000s	%
Coal-mining	192	46	64	16	158	38
Stones and clays	76	27	66	23	138	50
Iron mines	58	30	80	42	54	28
Foundries	11	29	14	39	12	32
Iron, steel, and metal goods	127	60	47	22	37	18
Mech. engineering	233	64	78	21	56	15
Electricity	56	56	24	24	20	20
Optical	25	67	7	14	5	15
Chemicals	33	25	18	14	80	61
Textiles	51	18	152	52	89	31
Paper	21	22	30	32	44	46
Mimeo. (printing)	80	70	8	7	26	23
Leather	17	36	18	36	14	28
Rubber	4	20	6	29	10	51
Timber	128	54	42	18	65	28
Musical goods	5	49	3	28	2	24
Food and drink	251	61	46	11	113	28
Clothing	82	64	30	24	16	13
Building	342	58	54	9	193	33
Water, gas, and electricity	41	43	31	33	23	24
Laundry	41	82	4	8	5	10
Total	1,874	48.6	821	21.3	1,160	30.1

Source: Lee (1978), 447.

On-the-job training was one element of this process. Apprenticeship, for example, played an important role in disseminating knowledge, though one which declined over much of the nineteenth century. Thus, in 1895, some 27.3 percent of the work force were qualified artisans (journeymen who had completed their apprenticeship). This represents a low point in the influence of the *apprenticeship* system, since the percentage had previously been much higher and was later to recover somewhat, reaching 33.6 percent by 1939. Industry, meanwhile, welcomed and promoted apprentice-workshops. The state also helped in this respect, in 1897, for example, with a law strengthening the traditional craft guilds and their educational functions.

(Stuttgart, 1984), 637–65, for a study of the diffusion of the puddling iron refining technique by means of internationally mobile puddlers in Western Europe over the first half of the nineteenth century.

Formal technical education was another effective means of imparting skills. A separate system of technical education developed in Prussia after 1806, consisting of three different levels. The first (lower level) taught artisans and skilled industrial workers practical knowledge. The second (middle-level) educated engineers. At the top level, polytechnical schools on a par with universities were founded to advance more theoretical knowledge. They became known as Technische Hochschulen (institutes of technology), the more famous of which were in Darmstadt, Karlsruhe, and Berlin. Non-Prussian institutes of technology followed the French model. In addition, from the 1860s on, vocational schools proliferated. As a result, nineteenth-century Germany developed a broad-based system of technical education, which may be said to have offset the failure of German industry to profit from English technological innovations of the late eighteenth century, which some contemporary observers argued was an important factor in Germany's comparatively late industrialization. Universities, finally, supplied important industrial inputs, the most noteworthy example being skilled chemists. All in all, there are strong hints that the educational system played its role so well that only unskilled labor was in surplus at the end of the nineteenth century, although exact comparative data are missing.

Living Conditions

What factors determined the living conditions of working people? The most important elements include stability of employment, threat of unemployment (job security), wages and salaries, working time, and working conditions.

For nineteenth-century Germany, we have some empirical information on all of the above. Although only approximations, the statistics help us understand how the living conditions of workers changed over the course of the nineteenth century.

Let us first look at employment, or rather, at unemployment. Recall that earlier in the century underemployment, as opposed to open unemployment, was the more typical status of laborers in slack times, a feature which reflects the prevalence of self-employment. In the second half of the century, however, dependent employment became the standard labor force situation, with unemployment as its "slack times" counterpart. In spite of a few sharp increases, unemployment was surprisingly low at the end of the nineteenth century, as table 34 suggests. Wages are another

Table 34: The Unemployment Rate in Germany (1887–1913) (in percent)

Year	Kuczynski I	Kuczynski II	Year	Kuczynski I	Kuczynski II	Galenson and Zeller
1887	0.2	1.0	1900	2.0	2.5	
1888	3.8	4.5	1901	6.7	7.2	
1889	0.2	1.0	1902	2.9	3.2	
1890	2.3	2.5	1903		2.7	47.0
1891	3.9	4.5	1904		2.1	3.6
1892	6.3	6.0	1905		1.6	3.0
1893	2.8	3.5	1906		1.2	2.7
1894	3.1	3.5	1907		1.6	2.9
1895	2.8	3.5	1908		2.9	4.4
1896	0.6	1.0	1909		2.8	4.3
1897	1.2	1.5	1910		1.9	3.5
1898	0.4	1.0	1911		1.9	3.1
1899	1.2	1.5	1912		2.0	3.2
			1913		2.9	4.2

Source: Pierenkemper (1987), 58.

important indicator. In general, income increases were relatively modest before 1850, and this in an economy that had very few wage-earners. Real wages fluctuated a great deal, but not because nominal wages fluctuated. The reason was that significant harvest variations caused food prices to fluctuate greatly, while food prices were a major factor in the nominal wage/cost of living ratio determining real wages. In the long run, however, nominal wages did grow, and thus real wages increased considerably, particularly after 1870. For working people, real income increased 20 percent between 1880 and 1900, probably somewhat less than that between 1900 and 1913 (see table 35).

A further source of increasing worker welfare was a steady reduction in working time. Workdays of fourteen to sixteen hours, six days a week were standard in the early nineteenth century, and were interrupted only by brief pauses for recreation. This amounted to workweeks of eighty to eighty-five hours.

These heavy work schedules declined, falling continuously and almost dramatically after the 1850s. By the eve of World War I, work weeks averaged about 40 hours throughout Germany. The decrease in the workload was in all probability related—both as cause and as effect of an increase in productivity. Table 36 offers an estimate of these improvements.

Table 35: The Growth of Real Wages in Germany (1850–1913) (1913 = 100)

Year	Kuczynski	Year	Kuczynski	Bry	Desai	Orsagh	Year	Kuczynski	Bry	Desai	Orsagh
1850	87	1870	76				1890	91	87	76	73
1851	79	1871	75	74	56	52	1891	90	84	74	70
1852	67	1872	79	79	63	59	1892	91	86	75	71
1853	63	1873	78	79	68	64	1893	92	87	80	78
1854	58	1874	77	78	66	61	1894	93	88	79	78
1855	55	1875	85	84	69	64	1895	94	89	80	78
1856	58	1876	81	78	66	62	1896	96	97	94	82
1857	73	1877	78	73	62	60	1897	96	96	92	86
1858	75	1878	83	77	67	65	1898	95	93	87	85
1859	73	1879	82	74	66	64	1899	98	96	93	89
1860	71	1880	78	70	63	61	1900	99	98	88	87
1861	60	1881	77	70	64	61	1901	97	95	90	89
1862	70	1882	80	75	69	66	1902	97	95	89	88
1863	76	1883	80	75	69	65	1903	98	96	90	89
1864	82	1884	85	80	71	68	1904	99	97	92	91
1865	78	1885	88	83	71	67	1905	98	98	91	89
1866	77	1886	90	85	71	68	1906	97	97	93	92
1867	66	1887	91	87	77	73	1907	100	101	94	93
1868	68	1888	92	89	76	72	1908	100	100	94	93
1869	75	1889	92	88	72	70	1909	99	99	92	92
							1910	98	99	94	93
							1911	98	98	94	95
							1912	96	96	96	96
							1913	100	100	100	100

Source: Pierenkemper (1987), 66.

Table 36: The Decline in the Number of the Hours Worked in Germany
(1860–1913)

Period	Average workday for industrial workers (in hours)	Average workweek for industrial workers (in hours)
Around 1860	14–16	80–85
1861–1870	12–14	78
1871–1880	12	72
1881–1890	11	66
1891–1895	10.5–11	63–65
1896–1900	10.5	61–63
1901–1905	10–10.5	59–61
1906–1909	10–10.5	58–60
1910–1914	10	54–60

Source: Pierenkemper (1987), 64.

In contrast to incomes and the work week (see graph 16), working conditions, which represent the "quality" of jobs offered, are rather difficult to measure. The reduction of working hours clearly made an important contribution to the improvement of working conditions. Other indicators point in the same direction, such as the declining number of per capita work accidents and the improved health of working people. Still, the degree to which these improvements benefited the working class is disputed even today, so that a fair judgment is very difficult to make.

Institutional Arrangements

In Germany, state intervention in labor market relations came early. In 1839, the Prussian government enacted a law banning children under fourteen from working at all and women from working in factories. Many more regulations followed, but proved difficult to enforce. Mandatory school attendance was an effective measure restricting daytime child labor in cities, but it was less effective in rural areas and child labor after school hours even in cities remained prevalent.

In the 1870s, the state began efforts to set up a social security system motivated by the desire to win and hold working-class loyalty. The first measure enacted provided coverage for work accidents (1881); then came the first step toward a state-sponsored health-care system and a state-managed pension scheme (1886). Coverage, however, was, even in 1914, far from universal. Attempts to

Graph 16: The Development of Welfare in Germany since the Mid-nineteenth Century: Income, the Work Week, and Unemployment

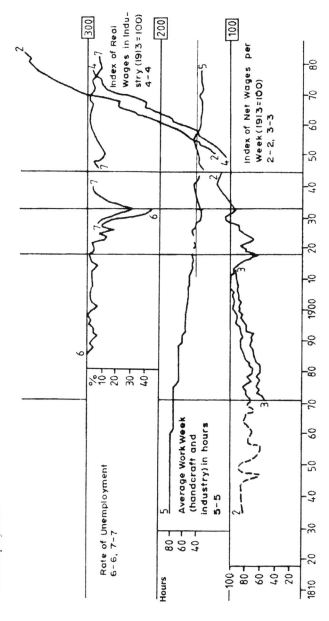

introduce a central labor administration first became successful after World War I, in 1927, when the Federal Unemployment Office was established.

These measures were part of Bismarck's strategy vis-à-vis Germany's growing labor movement, as more or less permanent trade unions began to spring up in the 1860s and 1870s. State laws in 1868 and 1869 lifted restrictions on trade union organization and unions boomed—along with the strike activity they helped to promote. The unions that emerged differed in strength and importance in the various branches of industry, but all played a role in the harsh struggles between employers and workers. An important step came in the 1890s when "industrial unions" were formed, i.e., unions that brought skilled and unskilled workers of a given branch into one organization. Their socialist orientation—they had close ties to the Marxist Social Democratic Party—made them appear more dangerous to middle-class and upper-class political leaders than they were in fact. By international standards, however, they were strong. With around three million members in 1914—and links with the Social Democrats, the German parliament's strongest party—they were the center of what was probably the world's largest labor movement.

In response to this impressive labor organization, employers created their own associations in the first decade of the twentieth century. In addition to labor disputes, these employers' organizations also dealt with questions of tariffs and customs duties as well as broader aspects of social policy. Although both employee and employer organizations originated from labor conflicts, they may have had long-run productivity-enhancing effects, since they were institutions that improved the flow of information between employers and employees, thus reducing the bases for mutual mistrust. More than one economist has suggested that if workers had proved unable to organize unions, employers, in their own interest, would have done it for them.[20]

20. R. Freeman and J. Medoff, *What Do Unions Do?* (New York, 1984). For a study suggesting employer acceptance of collective bargaining with unions by the 1900s, see H. Kaelble and H. Volkmann, "Konjunktur und Streik während des Übergangs zum organisierten Kapitalismus in Deutschland," *Zeitschrift für Wirtschafts- und Sozialwissenschaften* 92 (1972): 513–44.

Chapter Seven

MONEY AND BANKING

For a number of reasons banking was an important sector in the nineteenth-century German economy, mainly because of the key role of financial capital in the early stages of industrialization. In market economies banks act as financial institutions that bring together and synchronize decentralized savings and investment decisions of individual economic agents. The large and risky investments of railways and heavy industry between the 1840s and the 1870s could not be financed out of profits or from individual savings. Banks had to intervene. At first these were private bankers, family firms or partnerships with unlimited liability, but when their resources proved inadequate, these bankers founded joint-stock banks to do the job for them. Together they organized and financed the growth of Germany's "Leading Sector Syndrome" (see chapters 3 and 4), developing in the process what has come to be known as "universal banking" (or "mixed banking"), the combination of commercial bank deposit and loan business with investment banking activities.

This kind of banking led to the creation of very large banks. In 1913 the five big Berlin banks controlled, by themselves and through allied banks, an aggregate of around seven billion marks, about half of the total assets of all joint-stock universal banks. In that same year, the three largest German enterprises were banks, as were 17 of the largest 25![1] This represents a degree of bank prominence that we can find in no other industrial economy of the

1. See R. Tilly, "Banken und Industrialisierung in Deutschland: Quantifizierungsversuche," in *Entwicklung und Aufgaben von Versicherungen und Banken in*

world at this time. It is one of the most striking features of Germany's economy. Contemporaries were aware of the phenomenon. There was much public criticism of the power of banks and the dangers of concentration. In 1910, Jacob Riesser,[2] a director of one of the largest banks (the Darmstädter Bank), wrote a major work on the subject of the big banks in response to such criticism and as an attempt to demonstrate the banks' economic usefulness. At about the same time, a Marxist revisionist, Rudolf Hilferding, published an influential treatise on the big banks, *Finanzkapital*, which emphasized the great power of the banks over the economy as a whole.[3] The debate on the role of these banks has gone on ever since.

Structure of the Banking Sector

It is of great interest and importance to place the role of these big banks in proper perspective—the perspective of the economy and financial system as a whole. A first step is to examine the overall structure of Germany's financial development in the nineteenth century. Table 37 offers some of the relevant evidence, helping to identify three important features of Germany's financial structure.

The first has to do with the development of central banking and controls over the economy's money supply (see the entry "Banks of issue," row 1). In terms of total assets, the importance of this type of institution declined. The sum of total assets alone, however, does not capture the true importance of banks of issue. At mid-century, in most German states banknotes were regarded as a form of money with "public good" attributes, whose circulation was important for the economy's stability, very close to coins. Their issue was therefore strictly regulated by the states. In Prussia, the largest state, a government-controlled institution, the Bank of Prussia, enjoyed a near monopoly of note issue. In the 1870s, as we have already seen (chapter 3), that right was transferred to the

---

der Industrialisierung, ed. F. W. Henning, Schriften des Vereins für Socialpolitik (Berlin, 1980), 165–93.

2. Riesser's work was regarded in the United States as so authoritative that it was published as part of the documentation of the U.S. National Monetary Commission: J. Riesser, *The German Great Banks and Their Concentration in Relation to the Economic Development of Germany* (Washington, 1911).

3. R. Hilferding, *Das Finanzkapital* (Berlin, 1909). See also V. Wellhöner, *Großbanken und Großindustrie im Kaiserreich*, Kritische Studien zur Geschichtswissenschaft, vol. 85 (Göttingen, 1989).

Table 37: Assets of German Financial Institutions (1860–1913)
(in billions of marks)

Type of Institution	1860	1880	1900	1913
Banks of issue (Notenbanken)	0.95	1.57	2.57	4.03
Commercial banks (Kreditbanken)	0.39	1.35	6.96	22.04
Private banks (Privatbanken)	1.50	2.50	3.50	4.00
Saving banks (Sparkassen)	0.51	2.78	9.45	22.56
Credit cooperatives (Kreditgenossenschaften)	0.01	0.59	1.68	6.17
Mortgage banks (Hypothekenbanken)	0.09	1.85	7.50	13.55
Public land and mortgage institutions (Öffentliche Land- und Hypothekenbanken)	0.68	1.76	4.05	7.20
Life insurance companies (Lebensversicherungen)	0.07	0.44	2.42	5.64
Other insurance companies (andere Versicherungen)	–	0.35	0.83	2.05
Social insurance (Sozialversicherungen)	–	–	0.87	2.25
Other	–	–	–	0.98
Total	**4.25**	**13.5**	**40.5**	**91.00**

Source: R. Tilly, "An Overview on the Role of the Large German Banks up to 1914," in *Finance and Financiers in European History, 1880–1960*, ed. Y. Cassis (Cambridge, 1992), 93–112, here 96.

new central bank, the Reichsbank, which soon became the dominant bank of issue, regulator of the country's supply of cash and system of payments. The significance of this development lay in the fact that the Reichsbank had to be ready to redeem its notes in gold coin on demand and, hence, to concentrate on safe and highly liquid business. Other banks, on the other hand, thus excluded from the payments business, could and had to turn to more risky business, in particular, to the "mixed banking" operations mentioned earlier. The growth of the latter among German banks can thus be seen as a result of a division of labor between government-dominated institutions and profit-oriented commercial banks. If the latter got into trouble and became temporarily illiquid, they could count on the Reichsbank to help them; and this further encouraged the growth of "mixed banking."

A second feature of the German financial structure that is captured in table 37 is the great increase in total business transacted through institutions other than the joint-stock commercial banks: the mortgage banks and insurance companies, active in urban real estate, the credit cooperatives, which catered to craft workers and farmers, and above all the system of public savings banks, which attracted middle-class savings and served the credit needs of small business, both urban and rural. A further point worth making is that the private bankers, although in relative decline, were not of negligible importance, even in 1913 (see table 37, line 3). Taken together, these are grounds for caution when interpreting German financial development solely in terms of the great mixed banks.

The third feature worth remarking here concerns financial activities undertaken outside the banking system. Two kinds were important: the self-financing of non-financial firms, which by all historical accounts was by far the most significant source of industrial finance, between 1850–1914; and the issue and placement of securities (stocks and bonds) which were held by private investors. We have no direct evidence on the aggregate value of self-finance, but a comparison of line 1a and line 5 in table 38 suggests that its aggregate importance was not growing.

Table 38: Assets in Germany (1875–1913) (in billions of marks)

		1875	1895	1913
1a)	Total financial assets	44	98	252
1b)	(of financial institutions)	11	29	83
2	Real estate	54	52	97
3	Other real domestic assets	81	104	265
4	Other assets	7	14	25
5	Total assets	186	268	639

Source: Tilly (1992), 96.

Comparing line 1a and 1b, on the other hand, indicates that finance by security issue was growing, though much of this represented the public sector's borrowing. Direct evidence on securities in relation to total financial assets corroborates this.

1875–85 (average)	17.4 percent
1912–14 (average)	20.0 percent

International comparison, however, shows that, in this regard, Germany was well behind its main competitors, France, Great Britain, and the United States (figures for 1912–14):

France	37.4 percent
Great Britain	35.6 percent
United States	42.2 percent

This could reflect the fact that in Germany before 1914, the stock exchanges were subjected to restrictive regulation (Law of 1896) and relatively high taxes, which deflected business to German banks and also to foreign exchanges.[4] Space limitations make it impossible to pursue the question further here.

Contributions of Banks to Industrial Growth

Mixed banking emerged during Germany's "industrial break-through" between the 1840s and 1870s. Private bankers played a leading role in the organization and financing of the early railways, advancing funds, placing the railways' stocks and bonds with their own customers, and assuming directorships in those companies by virtue of their ability to mobilize proxy votes at shareholders meetings. As indicated above, railway finance proved to be a risky business, and led private bankers to found joint-stock banks with limited liability, so to speak as a permanent form of risk diversification. The same procedures were applied almost simultaneously to help get German heavy industry going in the 1850s and 1860s. It seems most likely that Germany's railways, iron foundries and rolling mills, and mines came into operation earlier than they would have, thanks to the readiness of private bankers to engage in mixed banking activities and to extend the same operating procedures to the joint-stock banks that they founded.

In the period between 1870 and 1914, Germany's big mixed banks went on to play the leading role in the financing and organization of large-scale enterprises, mainly in the form of joint-stock companies. Private bankers became secondary "players" in the game of industrial finance. The big banks developed close ties to the industrial enterprises. Sometimes this led to drastic action. In the 1870s, for example, after the "Gründerboom" had turned into crisis, a group of banks led by the Berlin Disconto-Gesellschaft

---

4. On this, see R. Tilly, "Universal Banking in Historical Perspective," *Journal for Institutional Theoretical Economics* 154 (1998): 7–32; on the Law of 1896, see C. Wetzel, *Die Auswirkungen des Reichsbörsengesetzes von 1896 auf die Effektenbörsen im Deutschen Reich, insbesondere auf die Berliner Fondsbörse* (Münster, 1996).

forced the Rheinish-Westphalian steel producers into a steel rail cartel, thereby preventing a round of cutthroat competition that would have threatened the banks' considerable stake in those companies.[5] About twenty years later, we find the big banks active in the reorganization of the electrotechnical industry, their efforts closely related to the huge risks involved in backing a potential loser. We find the Deutsche Bank, presumably because of its financial leverage, intervening sharply into family business policies.[6] Once the industry had stabilized—marked by the emergence of the two giants, A.E.G. and Siemens—the banks became less active, but in a critical phase they were important indeed.

Naturally enough, the capital-intensive industries—coal and steel, transportation, utilities, heavy engineering—remained the preferred playing field for the large mixed banks. Their activity centered particularly around reorganizations. They transformed older family enterprises into new joint-stock companies (for example, Hoesch Steel), merged existing companies, facilitated takeovers of smaller companies by larger ones, and financed simple expansions of existing companies, all by means of the issue and placement of new stocks and bonds. This was a cyclical business that involved considerable risk. Graphs 17 and 18 show the chronological pattern that characterized the period.

Note that from the 1890s on, the creation of new joint-stock companies slowed, while capital growth, as measured by new issues, continued, implying that it concentrated more among already existing companies. This may reflect the effects of the Companies Law of 1884, which restricted new share issues, but it could also reflect the profit-oriented strategies of the banks.[7] In any case, this was later to impede innovation, since new companies were more likely to innovate in order to be competitive.

5. The main companies involved were the Bochumer Verein, Krupp, and the Dortmunder Union. See on this U. Wengenroth, *Unternehmensstrategien und Technischer Fortschritt. Die deutsche und britische Stahlindustrie 1865–1895* (Göttingen, 1986).
6. On this, see Kocka (1969), 319–35; H. Neuburger, *German Banks and German Growth from Unification to World War I* (New York, 1977), esp. chap. 3; and R. Tilly, "Mergers, External Growth and Finance in the Development of Large-Scale Enterprises in Germany, 1880–1913," *Journal of Economic History* 42 (1982): 629–58.
7. The Companies Law of 1884 is dealt with by N. Reich, *Auswirkungen der deutschen Aktienrechtsreform von 1884 auf die Konzentration der deutschen Wirtschaft, in Recht und Entwicklung der Großunternehmen im 19. und frühen 20. Jahrhundert*, ed. N. Horn and J. Kocka (Göttingen, 1979). See also R. Tilly, "German Banking, 1850–1914: Development Assistance for the Strong," *Journal for Economic History* 15 (1986): 11352.

Graph 17: Joint-Stock Companies Founded between 1871 and 1913

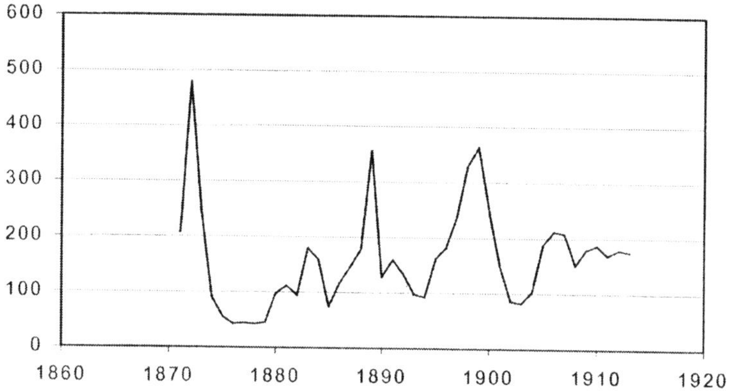

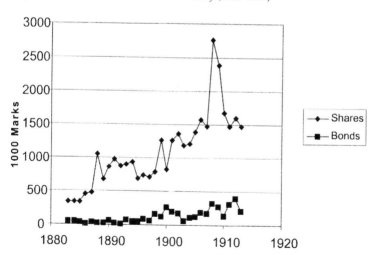

Source: W. Feldenkirchen, "Banking and Economic Growth: Banks and Industry in Germany in the Nineteenth Century and Their Changing Relationship during Industrialization," in *German Industry and German Industrialisation,* ed. W. R. Lee (London, 1991), 116–47, here 124.

Graph 18: Placement of Securities in Germany (1883–1913)

Source: Feldenkirchen (1991), 124.

One of the most striking features of German industrial finance in this period is the increasing presence of bankers as members of the boards of directors of industrial companies. This is another development furthered by the Law of 1884, for that law gave the supervisory board, elected by the shareholders, broad powers. It gave the banks a great potential for exercising influence over their industrial customers. Some historians have argued that this gave banks not only power, but also valuable inside information about their customers' financial position and motivated them to finance strategic, even if risky, investment projects. Other historians, however, have argued that such board seats did not necessarily convey much influence over industrial companies. As so often, more evidence is needed.[8]

Strictly speaking, however, none of this descriptive information on the mixed banks' activity really settles the issue of their contribution to German industrial growth. For that judgement we need to know what the performance of the industrial sector might have been without the mixed banks. One attempt to estimate this hypothetical value was made some years ago by two American scholars, Neuburger and Stokes.[9] They argued that German banks favored heavy industry at the expense of light industry, leading to inefficiency in the form of lower marginal returns on capital than would have been realized in a more competitive system. Another approach is to compare German capital allocation with that of other countries. One of the authors compared German performance with that of Britain, the hypothetical alternative financial system thus being the British one.[10] Taking the distribution of new issues of securities among the different sectors of the economy as an index of bank credit allocation, we find the differences as listed in the tables 39a and 39b. In these tables "yields" of the listed branches of the economy are measured by the estimated annual average rate of growth of the branch over the 1880–1913 period, and "risk" by the variance or standard deviation of those same series. The "shares in portfolio" represent the share of companies in those branches in the total issue of new shares on the Berlin stock exchange in the same period. Thus, "mining" grew in Germany, represented by issues of the Berlin stock exchange, at an

8. See, for example, Wellhöner (1989).
9. H. Neuburger and H. Stokes, "German Banks and German Growth, 1883–1913: An Empirical View," *Journal of Economic History* 34 (1974): 710–31.
10. Tilly (1986).

average annual rate of 4.13 percent, while 4.41 was the standard deviation of annual growth rates from that mean over the period (representing the risk of this investment). Shares issued by mining companies in the period amounted to 5.3 percent of the total issued on the Berlin stock exchange. Summing up the findings of table 39a, we find that not only did a very high share of the German banks' funds go to a small number of fast-growing and risky branches, but the efficiency of the distribution, as measured by the trade-off between risk and yield, was clearly greater in Germany compared to the numbers in table 39b, which represents the British performance. The portfolio being more efficient is an argument in favor of the mixed banks representing the German case. More research is needed here, however, and the finding just cited is certainly not the last word on the subject.

Table 39a: Estimated Asset Yields and Asset Shares in Bank Portfolio in Germany (1880–1913) (in percent)

Branch	nr.	Estimated yield	risk	Share in portfolio incl. sector 12	excl. sector 12
Mining	1	4.13	4.41	5.30	6.80
Quarrying	2	4.30	8.58	1.20	1.50
Metals	3	5.65	7.64	15.80	20.40
Engineering	4	6.01	6.34	10.50	13.50
Chemicals	5	5.98	3.85	4.80	6.20
Textiles	6	2.52	8.11	2.10	2.70
Wood and leather	7	3.62	7.75	2.20	2.90
Food and drink	8	2.81	3.91	3.20	4.20
Utilities	9	9.80	10.37	16.60	21.40
Construction	10	4.22	7.17	2.50	3.20
Transportation	11	5.63	3.19	10.40	13.40
Trade, finance, and insurance	12	3.50	2.27	23.80	
Miscellaneous	13	2.73	2.33	2.20	2.90
Portfolio				5.51	5.96
Standard deviation				3.09	

Source: R. Tilly, "German Banking, 1850–1914: Development Assistance to the Strong," *Journal of European Economic History* 15 (1986): 113–52, here 135.

Table 39b: Assumed Asset Yields and Asset Shares in British Capital Market Portfolio (1882–1913) (in percent)

Branch	Assumed Yield	Assumed Standard Deviation	Share in portfolio
1. Mining			3.33[1]
2. Quarrying	2.31	7.28	2.00[2]
3. Metals	2.55	9.05	1.43[1]
4. Chemicals	3.63	8.71	5.31
5. Engineering	3.00	9.84	10.60
6. Textiles	1.52	9.33	4.82
7. Food and drink	1.38	4.36	20.71
8. Gas, electricity, and water	4.86	3.89	5.16
9. Paper	5.04	10.78	1.76
10. Transport and communications	2.74	2.44	26.60[3]
11. Distribution	2.16	4.00	1.28
12. GDP	2.00	2.64	18.00[4]
13. Portfolio	2.45	8.20	100.00

Note: Actually covers years 1882–1905, 1907, and 1910–12.

1. Data on new issues of mining and metal production enterprises were merged as originally collected. Here they are assigned to coal and iron and steel as in the 1907 production census: 3:1.
2. As in first note with 1907 weight = 13/126 for coal mining.
3. Includes "Docks and Shipping."
4. Category "Other" in "Capital Created" statistics of IMM.

Source: R. Tilly, "Zur Finanzierung des Wirtschaftswachstums in Deutschland und Großbritannien, 1880–1913," in *Die Bedingungen in Vergangenheit und Zukunft*, ed. E. Helmstädter (Tübingen, 1984), 263–86, here 272.

Chapter Eight

ENTREPRENEURSHIP

In general parlance, "entrepreneurship" is a term used to describe the quality of enterprise leadership, though one which is difficult to define and difficult to analyze empirically. Perhaps it is for these reasons that entrepreneurship, though once an integral part of economic history, is no longer in fashion among the discipline's practitioners.[1] We include it here, however, because we believe it to shed important light on economic growth. We use the term here as a synonym for persons who had, or to whom were attributed, skills in running business enterprises.

By explicitly treating entrepreneurship, we obviously reject the view of Karl Marx who saw those who ran business enterprises as instruments of capital (or "Capital"), rather than as independent agents in the economic process. We are closer to Joseph Schumpeter, for whom entrepreneurs were quintessential for the development of capitalist, market economies. We do not follow Schumpeter in his tendency to equate entrepreneurs with innovation, however. Instead, following the example of Jürgen Kocka,[2] we wish to see entrepreneurship in the context of "economic backwardness" a

---

1. One of the standard U.S. journals started out as *Explorations in Entrepreneurial History* and became, with its new name, *Explorations in Economic History*, a major outlet for "cliometric" publications. In the second edition of *The Economic History of Modern Britain*, ed. R. Floud and D. McCloskey (Cambridge, 1994), the index lists "entrepreneurship," explains that it originated from the French word "to contract," and relates it to "managerial skills" or possibly "unusual managerial skills," but gives no page references; the book has no chapter on the subject. Nor do recent works on German economic history raise the question. The survey by Borchardt (1973) does not even mention the topic.

2. J. Kocka, *Unternehmer in der deutschen Industrialisierung* (Göttingen, 1975).

concept associated with the name of Alexander Gerschenkron.[3]
Gerschenkron ranked European nations in relation to the degree
to which their industrial development in the nineteenth century
lagged behind that of England, the first industrial country. The
greater the gap when those countries began to modernize, the
greater the need for substitutes for the gradual institutional
change and capital accumulation which had marked England's
early industrialization.

Germany was obviously a case in point. It created substitutes
for the missing institutions and capital. Thus, the lack of industrial capital led to the establishment of a highly effective banking
system centered around big, joint-stock, universal banks, which
allocated capital efficiently, probably at least as efficiently as
decentralized financial markets could have done (discussed in
chapter 7). Similarly, large enterprises, vertically integrated, diver-
sified and utilizing salaried managers, became much more typical
of Germany's dynamic industries than of Great Britain's counterparts, where family firms were relatively more important. Education and schooling were used to make up for Germany's economic
deficiencies and disadvantages in terms of skilled labor, resources,
technology and—a hypothesis—a supply of entrepreneurial families and traditions. The lack of entrepreneurship and individual
wealth no doubt inhibited economic growth. Recruiting practices
for entrepreneurial personnel were less developed, and traditional
obstacles that impeded a smooth transition, were stronger in Germany than in Britain.[4]

It must be stressed, however, that "backwardness" can also
apply to social, cultural and political development. We are under
no obligation to describe backwardness solely in economic terms.
Backwardness, that is to say, is a historical, not an economic concept. Overcoming backwardness does not refer only to economic
modernization. More than anything, the term refers to the transition of a traditional society to a bourgeois/capitalist society or to

3. A. Gerschenkron, *Economic Backwardness in Historical Perspective* (Cambridge,
1962); and for a critical assessment, see R. Sylla and G. Toniolo, eds., *Patterns of
European Industrialization in the Nineteenth Century* (London, 1991).

4. For an interesting attempt at comparative entrepreneurial history as an ele-
ment of economic growth, see C. Kindleberger, *Economic Growth in France and
Britain, 1851–1950* (Cambridge, 1964), chap. 6. For an excellent discussion of Anglo-
German differences in entrepreneurship, see H. Berghoff and R. Moeller, "Tired
Pioneers and Dynamic Newcomers? A Comparative Essay on English and German
Entrepreneurial History, 1870–1914," *Economic History Review* 47 (1994): 262–87.

a liberal-democratic system. In Germany, however, socio-political backwardness persisted well into the twentieth century, especially in comparison with Britain, France, or the U.S. This notion has been developed by German historians and sometimes called the German special path ("Sonderweg").[5] Keeping it in mind, in the rest of this chapter we examine three dimensions of German entrepreneurial history: social origins, traditional obstacles, educational qualifications and political influence.

Social Origins and Mobility

As we review some of the empirical evidence on this topic we note the importance of regional and sectoral differences. The transition from a pre-industrial to an industrial, factory-based economy naturally was smoother in the more advanced regions such as the Rhineland, and Saxony, where commerce and entrepreneurship were already important. In much of the rest of Germany, and particularly in its eastern half, this was not the case.

Aside from differences of geography, sectoral differences existed as well. Change was more striking and more comprehensive in "newer" industrial sectors such as heavy industry, electrical engineering, and chemicals. But there was a great amount of continuity in familial and social terms, especially in the West, where old, long-established families made their mark on the nascent industry: Stumm, Hoesch, Krupp, and Poensgen were all successful merchants in the eighteenth century and were able to form industrial dynasties in the nineteenth.

This rather mixed picture is described in a book about Berlin entrepreneurs by Hartmut Kaelble.[6] According to him, only one in three entrepreneurs inherited a business directly from their fathers. Nonetheless, three out of four were sons of businessmen, which is quite an extraordinary distribution compared with the entire population of Berlin at this time. Tables 40–42 illustrate his findings, which are based on experience in the early nineteenth century but also apply to the later period.

Kaelble's study draws on early-nineteenth-century experience; but other studies, including those which cover the later period,

---

5. H. Grebing, *Der "deutsche Sonderweg" in Europa 1806–1945. Eine Kritik* (Stuttgart, 1986); D. Blackbourn and G. Eley, *The Peculiarities of German History Bourgeois Society and Politics in Nineteenth-Century Germany* (Oxford, 1992).

6. H. Kaelble, *Berliner Unternehmer während der frühen Industrialisierung* (Berlin, 1972).

Table 40: Origins of Berlin Businessmen (father's profession)

Father's Profession	Absolute Numbers	% of total
Bankers	19	
Merchants	38	
Industrialists	39	
Total businessmen	**96**	**78**
Artisans	5	
Restaurant owners/innkeepers	2	
Landowners/renters	2	
Traders	3	
Total other businessmen	**12**	**10**
Civil servants/military	4	
Teachers	5	
Pastors/ministers	5	
Academics/professors	1	
Total civil servants and academics	**15**	**12**
Total known cases	**124**	**100**

Source: H. Kaelble, *Berliner Unternehmer während der frühen Industrialisierung* (Berlin and New York, 1972), 31.

Table 41: Professional Structure in Berlin and the Distribution of Social Backgrounds of Berlin Businessmen

Professional Group	Distribution of Social Backgrounds of Berlin Businessmen (in %)	Distribution of Professional Groups in Berlin in 1849 (in %)
Businessmen (big merchants, bankers, industrialists)	78	1
Other independent businessmen	10	14
Civil servants, pastors, teachers, doctors, pharmacists	12	4
Employees	–	81
Total	100	100

Source: Kaelble (1972), 37.

demonstrate roughly the same very specific recruitment pattern, in particular the predominance of upper middle-class origins. These empirical studies teach us to differentiate between time periods, branches of industry, and geographical regions. Nonetheless, the new business class was in fact not at all new, since it grew out of old commercial and business backgrounds. Thus, the creation of this group does not seem to indicate a high degree of upward social mobility, in contrast to the expectations we might

Table 42: Local Origin of Berlin Businessmen

| Birthplace | Date of Birth | | | |
	from 1799 in %	from 1800 to 1819 in %	after 1820 in %	Total in %
Berlin	41	31	52	40
Outlying area—Potsdam district	10	20	6	13
Distant areas (northeast): Mecklenburg, Province of Posen, Pommerania, Silesia, Frankfurt/Oder district	15	16	23	18
Distant areas (southwest): Province of Saxony, Saxon, and Thuringian areas	18	19	10	16
Other Prussian and German areas (borders of 1871)	15	11	6	11
Outside Germany (borders of 1871)	–	3	2	2
Totals	100	100	100	100
Number of cases	39	70	48	157

Source: Kaelble (1972), 20.

have from the concept of "relative backwardness." Most significantly, virtually none of the new entrepreneurs started out as a worker, either skilled or unskilled.[7] Nevertheless, one comparative difference which does fit the "backwardness" syndrome deserves mention here: in the second half of the nineteenth century, salaried managers were much more prevalent among successful business leaders in Germany than in Great Britain, where they played a much smaller role.[8] This reflected the greater strategic significance of large corporations for German industrial growth in this period, but it also has to do with the importance of what we call "traditional obstacles" to business success, a topic of the following section.

7. T. Pierenkemper, *Die westfälischen Schwerindustriellen 1852–1913. Soziale Struktur und unternehmerischer Erfolg* (Göttingen, 1979), 37–48; see also H. Kaelble, *Soziale Mobilität und Chancengleichheit im 19. und 20. Jahrhundert* (Göttingen, 1983), esp. 228–45.
8. Berghoff and Moeller (1994), 272, wherein proportions of 27.7 percent (German) and 7.3 percent are noted.

Traditional Obstacles

What about these obstacles? Systematic studies on this subject are lacking. What we can say, however, is that an anti-business tradition, related to the refusal to work for wages, prevented many aristocrats from becoming entrepreneurs. The same anti-entrepreneurial climate pervaded the *Bildungsbürgertum*, or educated middle-classes. For them, businessmen were ill-educated petty-bourgeois interested in materialistic values and profits, but not in the welfare of society or of the state. Civil servants, who enjoyed an extremely high status in society, were not concerned with entrepreneurship and competition, but with conformity, regulations, and widely accepted military standards. Therefore, German society never became business-friendly in the way the U.S. or Great Britain did.[9]

Nonetheless, the tendency to embrace business practice and culture became more and more apparent throughout the nineteenth century. Occasionally a successful businessman was rewarded with an aristocratic title (Werner von Siemens, for example), though this happened much less frequently than in Great Britain. Also, success in business became a symbol of national success and even a credential for a certain type of entrepreneur, more often, to be sure, for prominent merchants than for factory industrialists.

Increasingly, the old system came under pressure. Its absolute, inflexible rules helped destroy the corporatist system from within, as did the ideas of the Enlightenment and the work of the Prussian reformers from without. Religious orientation (Protestantism) continued to serve as a motivation in the search for economic success. Gradually, achievement replaced "ascription" as an instrument for social mobility. Geographical mobility increased, which in turn spurred the importance of economic factors. Scientific progress and the growth of the technical education system played a part, too. All in all, the social-cultural scene was changing deeply and quickly.

Relative backwardness also meant that Germans could learn and develop by looking at the gains made particularly in the area of technology by more advanced nations, such as England or the U.S. German entrepreneurs simply traveled to England or imported foreign workers. They were much more likely to do so than

9. For more details, see D. Blackbourn and R. J. Evans, eds., *The German Bourgeoisie* (London, 1991). But see M. J. Wiener, *English Culture and the Decline of the Industrial Spirit, 1850–1980* (Cambridge, 1981), for a similar interpretation of British culture from the late nineteenth century onward.

were British entrepreneurs, partly because Britain's industrial superiority must have made travel for industrial education purposes seem unnecessary. Meanwhile, British investors (Cockerill, Mulvany, and others) founded businesses in Germany, typically in those industries in which Britain enjoyed technological superiority. To some extent one could thus say that the Germans were not forced to be innovative, but could import the achievements of others, a successful borrowing that accounts for Germany's rapid industrialization and rise as an economic power. Nevertheless, it would be wrong to say that successful borrowing from abroad was a wholly passive, automatic process. In fact, it represented creative behavior which was, in the German case, actively facilitated by education.

Qualifications

Learning from abroad was an important part of the "catching-up" syndrome, causally related—as cause and effect—to the fact that German entrepreneurs enjoyed better formal education and were better traveled than their foreign competitors. As an example, the table 43 illustrates the distribution of the formal school qualifications of a sample of German heavy industrialists from the 1850–1914 period.

Of the 248 men sampled, 82 percent attended institutions of higher education, 71 percent graduated with a diploma, 16 percent had a technical education of some kind, and 2 percent went to commercial schools. If we compare development over time, we can see that education became increasingly important.[10] This contrasted sharply with comparable samples of British industrialists.[11]

In industry, the dominance of formally educated managers and executives was even stronger than in other sectors. By the end of the nineteenth century, their education had made them more important for the success of their firms than the traditional owner-entrepreneurs of the early industrial period. In fact, more than 50 percent of

10. J. C. Albisetti, *Secondary School Reform in Imperial Germany* (Princeton, 1983).
11. This striking difference was related to the greater importance in Germany of salaried managers, whose educational qualifications were much higher than those of German owner-entrepreneurs. The latter, like their British counterparts, depended more upon familial networks for success than managers. See Berghoff and Moeller (1994), 273. See also C. Erickson, *British Industrialists: Steel and Hosiery, 1850–1950* (Cambridge, 1960).

Table 43: Education of Westphalian Heavy Industrialists (according to management position)

	Founders	Supervisory Board Members	Directors	Total
Higher education				
w/o final examination	–	5	17	22
Progymnasium	–	–	1	1
Realschule	–	1	9	10
Höhere Bürgerschule	–	2	2	4
Rektoratsschule	–	1	3	4
Gymnasium	–	1	2	3
with final examination	9	28	104	141
Gymnasium	2	10	52	64
Realgymnasium	–	5	18	23
Oberrealschule	–	1	3	4
Not classified	7	12	31	50
Vocational school	3	2	27	32
Technikum	–	–	8	8
Gewerbeschule	3	2	18	23
Webschule	–	–	1	1
Commercial school	–	2	2	4
Total	12	37	150	199
No information	27	9	13	49
N	39	46	163	248

Source: T. Pierenkemper, *Die westfälischen Schwerindustriellen 1852–1913. Soziale Struktur und unternehmerischer Erfolg* (Göttingen, 1979), 51.

these managers had a formal education, so it seems likely that the German education system contributed to the development of German entrepreneurship (see table 44). It is sometimes argued that true managerial skills cannot be learned in schools, but are part of the character of talented people. Such an opinion, however, neglects the fact that in business there is much routine which must be taught and learned, and also that formal education can enhance the ability to absorb the less formalized on-the-job training. Therefore, we conclude that the technical education institutions which appeared in the nineteenth century were extremely important for the development of German industry.[12]

12. Some additional information can be found in C. E. McCelland, *State, Society and University in Germany 1700–1940* (Cambridge, 1980); F. K. Ringer, *The Decline of the German Mandarins: The German Academic Community, 1890–1933* (Cambridge, 1969); and K. H. Jarausch, *Students, Society and Politics in Imperial Germany* (Princeton, 1982).

Table 44: Fields of Study among Westphalian Heavy Industrialists (according to management position)

	Founders	Supervisory Board Members	Directors	Total
Vocational studies	5	12	105	122
Smelting	2	3	32	37
Mining	2	6	50	58
Engineering	1	3	22	26
Textiles	–	–	1	1
Natural sciences	–	1	4	5
Chemistry	–	1	3	4
Pharmacy	–	–	1	1
Trade	–	1	–	1
Other	3	9	5	17
History	–	2	–	2
Medicine	1	–	–	1
Mathematics	–	–	2	2
Law	2	7	3	12
Study without degree	1	1	4	6
No higher education	9	12	34	55
Total	18	36	152	206
No information	21	10	11	42
N	39	46	163	248

Source: Pierenkemper (1979), 60.

Political Influence

The concept of relative backwardness has often included arguments concerning the political influence of entrepreneurs, e.g., that the greater the degree of backwardness of an economy, the greater the entrepreneurial need for state support of its interests, and this applies to Germany as well.[13] In fact, the role of entrepreneurial political influence in Germany during the second half of the nineteenth century has often been discussed in German literature.[14] The various attempts at assessing that role have done so in three ways, namely,

13. See the arguments in Sylla and Toniolo (1991), esp. 16–18; and also the chapter by R. Tilly ("Germany"), 190–93.
14. For example, H.-J. Puhle, "Parlament, Parteien und Interessenverbände, 1890–1918," in *Das kaiserliche Deutschland. Politik und Gesellschaft, 1870–1918*, ed. M. Stürmer (Düsseldorf, 1970); H.-P. Ulmann, *Der Bund der Industriellen. Organisation, Einfluß und und Politik klein- und mittelbetrieblicher Industrieller im Deutschen Kaiserreich, 1895–1914* (Göttingen, 1976); H. Jaeger, *Unternehmer in der deutschen Politik (1890–1918)* (Bonn, 1967).

1. by investigating the political involvement of entrepreneurs in the legislative and executive branches of government, and in political parties;
2. by investigating certain political issues and determining whether entrepreneurs took them to heart, e.g., tariff policies, commercial regulations, social policy, and the like;
3. by looking more specifically at the representation of entrepreneurs in municipal, state, and national parliaments.

For the sake of convenience we confine our attention in this section to the third approach. Available evidence suggests that bankers, merchants, traditional business people and others played a more than negligible role in the Reichstag and state parliaments. In fact, throughout the nineteenth century, participation in politics was an important part of the bourgeois emancipation movement. Some business-people, such as Camphausen (a banker) or Hansemann (a merchant and later banker) attained prominent positions in the government of Prussia, and took part in the "Maerz-Regierung" of 1848. After the failure of the 1848 revolution, they left the government, and withdrew from politics. But with the creation of the Reichstag in 1871, a new avenue opened up which business leaders also utilized.

The data presented by Hans Jaeger confirm that a great number of entrepreneurs took part in politics and were elected to parliaments after 1871, peaking in the 1890s. Their numbers then fell from 27 percent of the legislators in the 1890–93 Reichstag to 17 percent in the 1912–18 Reichstag (the following tables 45 and 46 refer to the period 1890 to 1918). Nonetheless, this shift should not be taken as an index of decline from a position of great power and influence in Imperial Germany. What it does is to remind us to think about the definition of "entrepreneurship." For Jaeger employs a relatively broad concept of entrepreneurship, which leads him to present large numbers and high percentages compared to the statistics of most other authors. His definition of entrepreneurs includes industrialists, merchants, bankers, directors, and chief executives, but also passive capitalists (*Rentiers*), members of supervisory boards, representatives of trade unions and labor associations, as well as retired entrepreneurs. A narrower definition would show a less pronounced decline.[15] Moreover, there were

---

15. Thus, Berghoff and Moeller (1994), 280–81, cite 14.5 percent of all Reichstag members as an all-time high for entrepreneurial representation, whereas Jaeger's maximum is nearly twice as high (see table 44).

other avenues of political influence open to entrepreneurs interested in them, e.g., business associations, which were probably more important for specific business aims than the parliaments. Table 45 opens our discussion. It shows the decline just mentioned. In table 46 we see documentation of the obvious fact that the business world was not a monolithic one. For changes inside the structure of business clearly affected the policy aims of the parties and entrepreneurs alike. In this particular case, however, the marked decline of industry is not offset by a growth in the number of business leaders from other sectors. Trade and commerce produced a larger number of Reichstag members relative to industry, but declined in absolute representation, as did the financial sector. This doubtless reflects the non-business persons included in Jaeger's definition of entrepreneur.

A few other points can be made. First, business leaders were largely affiliated with the liberal party, either the National Liberal Party or the Left-Liberal Party. Second, they were relatively active as parliamentary members, more active as a rule than other professional groups, took part in more discussions, and by the turn of the twentieth century probably wielded influence well beyond the number of Reichstag seats they occupied. Finally, entrepreneurs

Table 45: Political Role of Businessmen

Legislative Period	Number of Businessmen	Businessmen as Percent of Legislators
1890–1893	107	27.0
1893–1898	90	22.8
1898–1903	90	22.8
1903–1906	96	24.3
1907–1912	84	21.1
1912–1918	68	17.1

Source: H. Jaeger, *Unternehmer in der deutschen Politik (1890–1918)* (Bonn, 1967), 47.

Table 46: Branches (number of businessmen)

	1890	1893	1898	1903	1907	1912
Industry	57	47	50	45	40	29
Trade/commerce	40	41	35	46	39	36
Finance	10	2	5	5	5	3

Source: Jaeger (1967), 53.

were also represented in the parliaments of the individual German states, though here too, their numbers were declining by 1900.

What the numbers cited here offer is an index of German entrepreneurial interest in public affairs, but not of their influence over government policy. For the latter, one has to look at the links between business leaders and the organized industrial and trade associations, such as the powerful Centralverband Deutscher Industrieller (Central Association of German Industrialists), in which business leaders were actively involved, which had considerable electoral influence, and which earned the title as "industry's private ministry."[16] From the perspective of the relative backwardness interpretation it is instructive to draw here once again on the comparative study by Berghoff and Moeller: they point out that in Britain entrepreneurial participation in parliament (the House of Commons) was much more frequent than that of their German counterparts, but that this related to the fact that in Great Britain parliament was much more important for government policy decisions than was the German Reichstag. Industrial and trade associations, in contrast, were weakly represented in Great Britain in comparison with Germany, where they not only conducted negotiations with the ministerial bureaucracy but were also strongly represented in the Reichstag.[17] This contrast reflected a difference in the maturity of parliamentary democracy in the two countries, but also a difference in the way business leaders approached politics. As Berghoff and Moeller write, "German businessmen's approach to politics rested upon a sharp distinction between their specific economic interests, which were carefully attended to, and general politics, which they preferred to leave to others."[18]

To sum up, recruitment and educational patterns in Germany fit the strategy of the industrial latecomer seeking to overcome backwardness. The evidence on political influence, on the other hand, does not seem to support the backwardness syndrome very clearly, though it does not contradict it. All in all, entrepreneurship opens up a chapter of German industrial history, without which that history remains badly incomplete.

---

16. See the classic study of this organization by H. Kaelble, *Industrielle Interessenpolitik in der Wilhelminischen Gesellschaft. Centralverband Deutscher Industrieller, 1895–1914* (Berlin, 1967).

17. Berghoff and Moeller (1994), 282.

18. Ibid., 283.

Chapter Nine

THE ROLE OF THE STATE

The role of the state in promoting German industrialization is a fascinating and important topic, but one which is fraught with methodological problems. Some of these were discussed earlier (in chapter 4), but they bear repeating. One derives from the nature of the historical source materials. Most of the evidence comes from government bodies engaged in or observing economic activities, and this material is likely to inflate the importance of the state's role. The use of alternative sources (e.g., the records of individual business firms) and theoretical models can attenuate this problem; but an exaggerated historical awareness of the state will tend to remain. A second problem concerns the ubiquity of connections between government and the private economy and the unintended economic consequences of state activity. Germany's emerging capitalist economy with its decentralized markets depended on a stable and trustworthy legal and political framework, and the government(s) which supplied it—or failed to supply it—required economic resources. Relevant examples spring to mind, such as an expanding judiciary, changes in the penal code, parliamentary elections, or spending on internal and external security—measures which had nothing to do with the explicit goal of promoting industrialization, but which could enhance or also offset the economic impact of other state activities.[1] A third problem has to do with the political ideology of German historians and resultant bias in the

---

1. Readers should note that with this point we implicitly enter a relatively new subfield of economics known as the "new institutional economics," wherein the concept of "transaction costs" borne by government plays a central role. To place German industrialization in that context properly would require another book. For

economic historiography toward an interpretation of the state as an important agent of industrialization. As we saw in chapter 4 above, this had to do with a hostility among economists and nascent economic historians toward nineteenth-century economic liberalism—or "Manchesterism" as it was sometime called—which powerfully affected historical studies of Prussian economic policies in the eighteenth and nineteenth centuries. For decades this generated literature expounding an extremely benign view of increasing state intervention in the economy. Eventually, a reaction came that led to more critical assessments of Prussian and German economic and social policies. Böhme, Wehler, and others called attention to the conservative political dimensions of those policies, but the interesting fact remains, that the weight and importance of the policies themselves as instruments for promoting industrialization were not called into question, but seen as means to achieve for Germany what one historian (Wehler) has termed "defensive modernization."[2] This is basically a tractable problem for traditional historical method; but the fact remains that those who study the question of German industrialization, will frequently have occasion to draw on secondary works which contain such bias. In the rest of this chapter it should be kept in mind.

Mercantilist Traditions and Periodization

The growing acceptance of economic liberalism as an ideology over the first half of the nineteenth century should not blind us to the continuing importance of what some historians call "mercantilist traditions" among German economic policymakers. According to one historian, three phases marked the nineteenth century.[3] A first phase of dominant mercantilism, marked by an active state responding to a lack of private entrepreneurship, came to an end in the 1840s. The tradition was exemplified by Upper Silesia, with

an introduction, see O. Williamson, *The Economic Institutions of Capitalism* (New York, 1985).

2. In a sense, the reaction goes back to the work of E. Kehr, *Der Primat der Innenpolitik* (Berlin, 1965), but more recent apostles are H. Böhme, *Deutschlands Weg zur Großmacht. Studien zum Verhältnis von Wirtschaft und Staat während der Reichsgründungszeit 1848–1881*, Cologne, Berlin, 1966; and H.-U. Wehler (1987–95).

3. C. Trebilcock, "Germany," in idem, *The Industrialization of the Continental Powers, 1780–1914* (London, 1981).

state-owned and managed iron works, and by the Saar region with state-owned coal mines.

The second period lasted from the 1840s to the 1870s and was typified by autonomous economic forces, the emergence of a free-market economy, and the sponsoring of private initiatives, e.g., with the help of state subsidies (as in railway-building). The ascendancy of economic liberalism, however, met resistance. Thus, while in 1848 the Frankfurt parliament sought to sweep all vestiges of the old order aside by preparing a uniform German commercial code (Allgemeines Handelsgesetz), a separate Artisans' Convention met in Frankfurt at the same time and demanded precisely the opposite. Such ambivalence persisted over the following decades. On the one hand, the Prussian government liberalized coal mining regulations and became more willing to grant concessions to joint-stock companies with limited liability; and by the end of the 1860s occupational freedom had become established in almost all German states. This was also a period marked by the liberalization of Germany's foreign trade (see also chapter 10). Finally, in 1870 the right to form incorporated business firms with limited liability was freed from government restraints. On the other hand, some state control of the economy continued. Saar coal mines, for example, remained under the control of Prussian bureaucrats, while in Upper Silesia, those same bureaucrats controlled blast furnaces, puddling ovens, and coal mines.[4]

In the 1870s, a third period began, marked by a sharp turn toward protectionism, increased interventionism, and the birth of what has been termed "organized capitalism."[5] The state centralized controls over the currency, established a central tariff system, and gave itself new powers to regulate economic activity. At the same time, the Empire saw the birth of social insurance, collective bargaining between representatives of capital and labor, and the spread of competition-inhibiting institutions such as cartels.

Looking back at this brief outline, we can say that the triumph of liberalism as the effective ideology of German economic policy in the third quarter of the nineteenth century was a limited one.

4. See Henderson (1958).

5. H. A. Winkler, ed., *Organisierter Kapitalismus. Voraussetzungen und Anfänge* (Göttingen, 1974); see also W. R. Lee, "Economic Development and the State in the Nineteenth Century in Germany," *Economic History Review* 41 (1988): 346–67.

"New" Economic Policies

We turn, then, to a number of specific measures which characterized the role of the German State in the economy during the latter
part of the nineteenth century. We skip over the 1850s and 1860s
and focus attention on the changes which began in the 1870s—
changes which some historians have seen as seismic shifts in the
political landscape connecting state and economy.[6] Before turning
to the policies themselves, however, it will be useful to look at the
historical context. What was changing? First of all, the short-run
change from the euphoric phase and boom which came in the
early 1870s, especially after the Franco-Prussian War of 1870–71, to
the crisis of 1873 and severe depression that followed, strengthened the demands of economic interest groups for state-sponsored
protection from competition and economic risks. The related and
continuing fall of staple prices (especially of grains) reflected an
intensified international competition that e.g., turned even the
East Elbian landowners from free traders into protectionists. Second, the advent of parliamentary democracy based on universal
manhood suffrage which came with the founding of the Kaiserreich, created a central government more responsive to economic
interest groups than had hitherto existed. Third, the new Reich
government centralized tariff policy and control over the currency,
making both of those policy areas more responsive to political con-
stituencies. Fourth, industrialization, urbanization, and mobility
produced unprecedentedly, large concentrations of working-class
populations whose social problems—e.g., working and housing
conditions—thus became more visible. Fifth, liberal laws of association facilitated—along with the urban concentration already
mentioned—the formation of labor organizations and strike movements, and stimulated fears of social unrest. A longer-run kind of
change which began at about this time involved the development
of science-based industries increasingly dependent on public educational and research facilities.

Such a context was propitious for the growing government
intervention of the period. Following a suggestion of Thomas

---

6. W. Abelshauser speaks of a "new social regime of production," by which he
means the advent of science-based industry and related organizational patterns,
while H.-U. Wehler sees the birth of the "corporatist interventionist state." See W.
Abelshauser, "Umbruch und Persistenz: Das deutsche Produktionsregime in historischer Perspektive," *Geschichte und Gesellschaft* 27 (2001): 503–23; and Wehler
(1987–95), 1266.

Wellenreuther, however, it is important to note at this point that (a) no large-scale dismantling of the emergent capitalist economy came about or was even projected, and, more importantly, that (b) among the most important socio-political groups of the Kaiserreich, there was no political constituency for the policies of economic liberalism.[7] Thus, the erstwhile free-trade oriented East Elbian Junker were defenders of private property in land, but in the 1870s they sought state protection both from creditors in the market for land mortgages and from overseas competitors in their product markets. Industrialists such as the leaders of heavy industry, meanwhile, espoused competitive labor markets but preferred protected product markets to competitive ones. Urban workers, finally, paid lip service to socialist doctrines, but in practice they favored reforms "within the system" such as government protection of labor unions, social insurance, rent control, and so on. What emerged from this context was a German variant of "mixed," or "Welfare Capitalism." In order to get a sense of that system's flavor, we now look at a short selection of policies associated with the Reich government's first chancellor, Prince Otto von Bismarck.[8]

Nationalization of the Railways

One of Bismarck's major policy aims was to make the imperial government, the Reich financially independent of the several German states. The well-known fact that railways were important sources of revenue for the states motivated Bismarck to the attempt to create a nationwide railway system under Imperial government ownership. In 1873 a Reich office was set up to administer the Alsace-Lorraine railways and enforce imperial laws that affected other railways in Germany. In short, the office's goal was to bring the entire system under central government control. In March 1874, and April 1875, the office sent two memoranda to the German parliament, the Reichstag. The stated purpose of the memoranda was to strengthen the power of the Reich government on these issues without actually nationalizing the railways. The memoranda faced so much criticism that Bismarck had them withdrawn.

---

7. T. Wellenreuther, "Die Infragestellung des ökonomischen Liberalismus in Deutschland von ca. 1870 bis 1913," in *Geschichte der Wirtschaftspolitik*, ed. R. Tilly (Munich and Vienna, 1993), 69–103.

8. W. O. Henderson, *The Industrial Revolution on the Continent: Germany, France, Russia 1800–1914* (London, 1967), 44–74.

Further initiatives by Bismarck got nowhere. In 1876 the Reichstag passed a law authorizing negotiations between the Reich and Prussia concerning sale of the latter's railways; but the law remained a dead letter.

Bismarck's most effective response, then, was to negotiate the nationalization of Prussia's privately owned railways, beginning in 1878—after the plans for creating a truly national system under imperial ownership had proved unrealizable. The purchase of the Prussian railways was not wholly unwelcome to private stockholders, for the crisis of the 1870s had lowered freight revenues and depressed stock prices. In long-run terms, the state takeover certainly proved important in a fiscal sense (for decades the railway revenues were the single most important source of the Prussian state's income), though whether it was an efficient economic solution remains an open question.[9] However well this arrangement may have worked for Prussia, it did not serve as a springboard to full nationalization, for the individual German states were too interested in holding onto their own main source of revenues. This whole episode, nevertheless, is a good reminder of the importance of federalism in late-nineteenth-century Germany. In this case it probably had negative consequences, since a truly nation-wide system of railways could have offered considerable savings through coordination of train traffic and of investment in fixed plant and equipment. The distribution of benefits from such a hypothetical alternative, however, would have depended on the aims of whoever controlled it.

Fiscal and Tariff Policy

Revenues were also at the heart of Bismarck's tariff policy. As depression deepened after 1873, industrial and agrarian interest groups organized and clamored for protective tariffs against foreign producers, especially of iron and grain (see chapter 5). In economic terms cone could call this "the demand for protection." The "supply of protection" was Bismarck's (and the Reich government's) interest in revenues.[10] The Reich government no doubt in

9. See on this R. Fremdling, "Freight Rates and State Budget: The Role of the National Prussian Railways, 1880–1913," *Journal of European Economic History* 9 (1980): 21–39; and D. Ziegler, *Eisenbahnen und Staat im Zeitalter der Industrialisierung*, Vierteljahrschrift für Sozial- und Wirtschaftsgeschichte, Bd. 127 (Stuttgart, 1996).

10. See on this formulation K. Borchardt, "Protektionismus im historischen Rückblick," in *Der neue Protektionismus*, ed. A. Gutowski (Hamburg, 1984), 17–47.

some sense "needed" more revenues at this time, e.g., to cope with rising military expenditures, but the main point was the strengthening of the Reich relative to the states. In any case, the general election of 1878 sent a protectionist majority to the new Reichstag. In July, 1879, a mildly protective tariff was passed. This was an important step away from economic liberalism. Initially, however, Bismarck's own interest was in revenues, in "financial duties," and not protective duties. And he was successful. The 1879 schedules were low enough to permit a high volume of imports to enter the country and thus to generate revenues, at least in the intermediate run.

In longer-run perspective, however, Bismarck and the Reich were not so successful. Two important limitations emerged. First, an amendment to the tariff law, written by an aristocrat, von Franckenstein (and thus called "the Franckenstein clause"), capped the Reich's share in tariff revenues at 130 million marks per year and called for the rest to be redistributed among the German states. Once again, we see here the importance of federalism at work. Second, once the tariffs came into force, they took on their own momentum. For retaliation of foreign countries led to tariffs on German products and encouraged economic interests in Germany to press for still higher duties. As we have seen (in chapter 5), they were forthcoming. The financial problems of the Reich, in fact, remained largely unsolved right up to World War I.[11]

Social Policy

Since the 1870s, the German state and its political leaders were confronted with the "social question" i.e., the need to harmonize the social interests and aspirations of the growing industrial working class with those of the rest of German society. These interests and aspirations were rather different from the question of "pauperism" which had marked the early nineteenth century. The increasingly urban and industrial working class was more concentrated, probably more homogeneous in its social condition and wants than the rural poor had been earlier. Certainly it was more visible as a political interest. A laissez-faire liberal approach to the problems at hand—of low wages, the risk of unemployment, overcrowded housing, and sickness—was felt by much of the upper

---

11. They were inextricably connected to the political and financial structures of the individual states, especially Prussia with its Three-Class-Voting system. See P.-C. Witt, *Die Finanzpolitik des Deutschen Reiches, 1901–1913* (Lübeck, 1970).

and middle classes to be dangerous, likely to polarize and possibly destabilize German society.

It is important to recognize, as was indicated earlier, that workers themselves had taken steps to mitigate their problems, through friendly societies, cooperatives, and then through the more militant socialist labor unions and political parties. But this was precisely what Bismarck and other political leaders hoped to prevent. Besides the "stick"—the oft-cited "Socialist Law" of 1878 which virtually outlawed Social Democratic activities—they used the "carrot." By this is meant the broad-based program of social insurance that Bismarck hoped would roll back the influence of the socialists over the working class.

About the same time as the Socialist Party was disbanded under the Coalition Law of 1876 (not to be confused with the Sozialistengesetz of 1878, which forbade any kind of socialist activity), Bismarck drafted a bill providing for compulsory state insurance for the sick, accident victims, and the elderly. As is well-known, these measures were revolutionary for the time, and were implemented earlier in Germany than in any other country. The Health Insurance Law, enacted in 1881, covered blue-collar workers and other working-class groups. By 1889, 5.5 million workers were insured under the new law. The system was run by decentralized organizations, which were a species of semi-public cooperative with a high degree of autonomy, were partly staffed by working-class representatives, and which saw to it that employers paid two-thirds of an employee's contribution, leaving the latter to pay the remaining one-third. Benefits included free medical services and weekly payments during the period of illness.

A year later, the Reichstag enacted an accident insurance law, which covered over 13 million people in 1889. The employers bore the entire costs of the measures, while funds were raised by newly created special associations, which were organized on a regional basis. In 1888, 15.6 percent of all accidents were fatal. Under the plan, a widow received a burial grant and a weekly pension, as well as additional allowances for dependent children.

Old-age and disability pensions appeared in 1887. Workers and employers each paid 50 percent of contributions for the pension funds, while the government added 50 marks per year per individual. That amount was increased in 1899. By then, pensions were being paid at the age of 70, and any individual who could no longer work received disability pensions on request.

Certainly, employers complained about the high costs of the welfare system, which they largely bore. By 1889, 14.5 million marks were paid for accident claims and 71 million for illness benefits; employers carried one-third of these costs. Meanwhile, socialists and union leaders complained about insufficient benefits and high contributions for workers. They called for payment of pensions at age sixty-five (since the average life span was not so high in those days, and fewer people lived to celebrate their seventieth birthday). Besides, 125 marks per year was a very small amount, barely enough to survive.

Nonetheless, the fledgling welfare system was in many ways a great achievement, since it gave workers a feeling of security and offered them some protection against the economic effects of old age and related calamities. To Bismarck's chagrin, however, the reform completely failed to weaken the socialist movement. In fact, the socialists polled 500,000 votes in the 1884 Reichstag elections, and 1.5 million six years later. The Anti-Socialist Laws were allowed to lapse in 1890 after Bismarck's resignation. However, the social security system remained in place, even if against the wishes and unsuccessful efforts of industrialists. It is likely that the state-sponsored system provided insurance on a scale which private initiatives—discouraged by Bismarck's measures—would have only achieved, if at all, much later.

This brief survey by no means exhausts the ways in which government and public policy affected the German economy in the second half of the nineteenth century. One important omission deserves mention here, however: the role of local government. Its importance lay in the fact that local government supplied most of the infrastructure and public services—water, sanitation, policing, fire protection, transportation facilities, etc—upon which daily life and indeed the very functioning of the economy itself depended. Control over local government lay largely in the hands of local elites and local economic interests, who operated via a few civil servants and the quasi-parliamentary bodies elected on the basis of an extremely narrow suffrage. Nevertheless, municipal governments in Germany's rapidly growing cities proved responsive to popular needs, and willing and able to provide an increasing array of qualitatively improving services.[12] This expansionism lay

12. On this, see, among others, J. Reulecke, *Geschichte der Urbanisierung in Deutschland* (Frankfurt am Main, 1985); T.-Y. Kwack, "Die Entwicklung von Kommunalunternehmen in Deutschland im 19. und frühen 20. Jahrhundert—unter

behind the rapid growth of local government spending in Germany in the second half of the century. By 1913 its share in Net National Product was over 6 percent—a larger share that that of the Reich! In consequence, on the whole, the infrastructure of Germany's big cities had become, by 1914, quantitatively and qualitatively comparable with the best-served cities anywhere in the world.[13] To some extent, this achievement reflected the responsiveness of local governments to local economic interests; but to some extent the changes referred to came at the initiative of local political leaders and civil servants, and not infrequently at the expense of important local economic interests.[14]

Let us sum up the chapter, then, in two points. First, governments had a non-negligible impact on the economy, both quantitatively—seen as a part of consumption and investment—and qualitatively—seen as a means for providing incentives for private economic actions, or for reducing socio-political conflict. It is not probable that private agents, by means of voluntary cooperative efforts, could have achieved equivalent results. Second, the activity of the state in the nineteenth century was not a constant, but changed over time, reflected the shifting economic, social and political structures in Germany. In some areas and at some times, policy clearly reflected powerful economic interests; but in other areas and times, particularly where interests were diffuse, policy could reflect the judgement and initiative of political leaders and high civil servants.

besonderer Berücksichtigung finanz- und sozialpolitischer Aspekte" (Ph.D. diss., University of Münster, 1989); also M. Hühner, *Kommunalfinanzen, Kommunalunternehmen und Kommunalpolitik im Deutschen Kaiserreich*, Münsteraner Beiträge zur Cliometrie und quantitativen Wirtschaftsgeschichte, vol. 6 (Münster, 1998); W. Krabbe, *Kommunalpolitik und Industrialisierung* (Stuttgart, 1985).

13. See J. Brown, "Coping with Crisis? The Diffusion of Waterworks in Late-Nineteenth-Century German Towns," *Journal of Economic History* 48 (1988): 307–18; also R. Tilly, "Städtewachstum, Kommunalfinanzen und Munizipalsozialismus in der deutschen Industrialisierung. Eine vergleichende Perspektive 1870–1913," in *Die Stadt als Dienstleistungszentrum. Beiträge zur Geschichte der Sozialstadt in Deutschland im 19. und frühen 20. Jahrhundert*, ed. J. Reulecke (St. Katharinen, 1995), 125–52.

14. On this, once again, see Reulecke (1985); see also Tilly (1995).

Chapter Ten

THE INTERNATIONAL ECONOMY

In the second half of the nineteenth century, the German economy became an increasingly important part of an expanding and increasingly integrated world economy. German foreign trade expanded enormously (with an annual growth rate of over four percent!), capital and labor flowed out of and into Germany and all of these movements were accompanied by flows of information on new technologies. A variant of economic globalization, to use today's phrase, was at work here, and the German economy was responding to it. It is in the nature of the relationship that the international economy was more important for the German economy than vice-versa. In this chapter we thus focus less on Germany than in previous chapters, discussing more generally the international economy, particularly trade and capital flows. We begin with some comments on international trade in the middle decades of the nineteenth century, then move to a closer discussion of Germany's part in its subsequent development through 1914, take up briefly the problem of agrarian protectionism, and conclude with a survey of foreign investment.

International Trade at Mid-century

At mid-century, Britain still dominated the international economy, as it had for at least 50 years. British leadership in trade reflected the country's head start in industrial development, for it was above all the new technologies of industrialization which created new products and new incentives for trade.[1] British dominance was decreasingly true of trade in Europe, however, as the Continental "core" countries began to successfully imitate and adopt Britain's superior industrial technologies and compete with British exports. World trade did not suffer on this account, however, for Britain adjusted to this competition by finding new markets for its exports on the European periphery and overseas. Meanwhile, industrialization in Europe not only stimulated exports but raised incomes and thus import demand as well. Thus, British trade with Europe need not have been falling in absolute terms. Moreover, industrialization also produced railways and steamships, and these led to falling transportation and shipping costs that gave a tremendous impetus to the growth of an international market for grains—one of the more important features of the international economy of these years.

Thus, the strong growth of international trade in these middle decades of the nineteenth century had as their primary motor the thrust of industrialization and the new technologies that came with it. Trade growth, however, also depended on another set of forces, related, but distinct: the liberal economic policies of the period, buttressed by the willingness of the most important economies to adhere to a system of currency convertibility at fixed exchange rates. We take these points up in turn.

Trade liberalization swept across Europe from the 1840s to the 1860s. The free-trade era was initiated by British tariff reductions in the 1840s, after the repeal of the Corn Laws. Its diffusion was powerfully aided by the Anglo-French Cobden-Chevalier Treaty (1860), for France and Britain together accounted for a large share of world trade, and their agreement stimulated imitators. The treaty was soon followed by many similar agreements between many European countries, e.g., the Franco-Belgian treaty of 1862, which served as a model for still more openness.

Adherence to an international regime of fixed exchange rates was at first based on silver and on gold currencies. The gold standard was later in coming. Great Britain had slid onto it in 1816, but most of the Continental countries first went over to gold in the 1870s, after the new German Empire had done so. The point being made here is that the commitment of many countries to maintain the external value of their currencies became apparent well before

---

1. For more on this interpretation, see S. Pollard, *Peaceful Conquest: The Industrialization of Europe, 1760–1970* (Oxford, 1981).

universal acceptance of the gold standard; and that commitment sufficed to encourage international trade.

The growth of international trade can be illustrated by table 47. The table, however, actually underestimates the expansion of trade in absolute terms, since it measures the value of exports per capita (excluding the effects of population growth).

Table 47: Value of Exports per Capita in European Areas (constant U.S. dollars)

	1820	1840	1860	1880	1900
Britain	3.6	7.25	20.7	31.0	36.2
Western Europe	1.7	3.2	7.3	14.8	25.9
Rest of Europe*	0.9	1.3	2.8	4.3	5.9

*Russia, Balkans, Greece, Turkey, Italy, Spain, Portugal.

Source: A. S. Milward and S. B. Saul, *The Economic Development of Continental Europe 1780–1870* (London, 1977), 471.

Trade Expansion, 1870–1914

Between the 1870s and 1914, world trade continued to grow. Trade in manufactured goods more than tripled, and Western Europe enjoyed the lion's share of its expansion. As table 48 illustrates, not all European nations benefited equally from the trade, to be sure. Germany's share of world trade in manufactured goods expanded dramatically, from 19.3 percent in 1880 to 26.6 percent in 1913. In contrast, France and Britain registered a relative decline. No reliable

Table 48: Shares of World Exports of Manufactured Goods among European Countries (1880–1913) (in percent)

	1880	1899	1913
France	22.2	14.4	12.1
Germany	19.3	22.4	26.6
Belgium and Luxembourg	5.0	5.5	5.0
Switzerland	n.a.	4.0	3.1
Sweden	0.8	0.9	1.4
Austria-Hungary	8.0*	n.a.	5.0
Britain	41.4	33.2	30.2

*This figure is approximate.

Source: Milward and Saul (1977), 473.

statistics are available for Germany before 1880, but its share in 1860 must have been below the 19.3 percent recorded for 1880.

Britain's share declined because of increasing competition and the spread of industrialization equipped with the newest technology. France's share declined, in part because its population—in contrast to those of Germany or Britain in this period—ceased to grow after 1870, and in part no doubt thanks to its stronger commitment to agriculture. Nevertheless, this differential export performance does raise the question of international competitiveness. For instance, the French and British "export structure" was strongly oriented toward textiles, but demand for these commodities no longer grew as fast as before, and where it continued to grow, other nations were self-sufficient. Germany, meanwhile, specialized in steel, chemical, and machinery exports. Germany was competitive because of its lower costs of production. This was partly a matter of lower wages, and Germans doubtless enjoyed a lower standard of living than their French and British counterparts. Around the turn of the century, indeed, the British government used this argument to blame Germany for "social dumping"! In addition, however, German industry had higher productivity because of better trained human capital resulting from its excellent educational system, and in some sectors because of more modern plant and equipment, which gave it a technological advantage.

The point hinted at here can be generalized: the relative export performance of countries resulted not from overall cost differences alone, but from the distribution of resources allocated to three different types of export sector, corresponding to:

1. fast-growing sectors (machinery and transportation equipment);
2. stable sectors with stable shares in trade (metals and chemicals); and
3. declining sectors (textiles).

Table 49 summarizes the story. Comparatively, Germany was doing better than France. Its share of expanding world trade totaled 16.9 percent, compared to France's 10 percent, while 49.5 percent of Germany's total trade fell into the contracting category, compared with 74.4 percent of France's total trade.

In geographic terms, Germany's great advantage was its ability to penetrate the nearby markets of close neighbors, especially Russia, Austria-Hungary, and Italy. Railway construction in those

Table 49: Shares of Exports of Manufactures by Groups (1913) (in percent)

	Germany	France	Italy	Belgium and Luxembourg	Switzer- land	Sweden
Expanding	16.9	10.0	7.6	9.3	11.8	18.8
Stable	33.6	15.6	8.4	29.9	11.3	35.9
Contracting	49.5	74.4	84.0	60.8	76.9	45.3

Source: Milward and Saul (1977), 473.

regions made these markets readily available to German steel, machinery, and even coal companies. Germany's exporting industries boomed because the distribution of markets and products created a high income elasticity of demand for German products.

Although Germany did not neglect South-American or Near-Eastern markets, its strength clearly lay in European trade. We can pursue the point further with some data on exports and imports. These data show the four leaders of world trade in 1913 to be the U.K., the U.S., Germany, and France (see table 50). The U.K. led with 15 percent, with Germany at 13 percent, the U.S. at 11 percent, and France at 8 percent (only half of the British share).[2]

Table 50: Foreign Trade of the Great Powers in 1913

	Export Bill. Dollars	Export Share (in %)	Import Bill. Dollars	Import Share (in %)	Foreign Trade Bill. Dollars	Foreign Trade Share (in %)
Great Britain	2.6	14	3.2	16	5.8	15
U.S.	2.4	13	1.8	9	4.2	11
Germany	2.4	13	2.6	13	5.0	13
France	1.3	7	1.6	8	3.0	8

Source: G. Hardach, *Deutschland in der Weltwirtschaft 1870–1970* (Frankfurt am Main, 1977), 99.

Export-regions were quite different. Germany exported 75 percent of its goods to Europe (France 70 percent, the U.S. 60 percent, and Britain 35 percent). But Germany, Britain, and the U.S. were much closer in terms of imports, most of which came from Europe (see table 51).

2. W. Fischer, *Die Weltwirtschaft im 20. Jahrhundert* (Göttingen, 1979); G. Hardach, *Deutschland in der Weltwirtschaft 1870–1970* (Frankfurt am Main, 1977).

Table 51: Regional Distribution of the Foreign Trade of the Great Powers in 1913 (in percent)

	Exports to			Imports from		
	Europe	North America	Other Continents	Europe	North America	Other Continents
Great Britain	35	10	55	44	24	32
U.S.	60	17	23	48	8	44
Germany	75	8	17	54	17	29
France	70	7	23	53	11	36

Source: Hardach (1977), 99.

Let us look for a moment at German trade alone. German efficiency, as well as the increasing size of the German economy, made Germany one of the world's leading traders by the turn of the twentieth century. The index of volume expanded from 4 or 5 in 1835, to 100 in 1913. From 1880 to 1913, the value of foreign trade went from about 3 billion marks to 9 or 10 billion (see graph 19).

Graph 19: German Foreign Trade in Quantity (1835–1913) and Value (1880–1913)

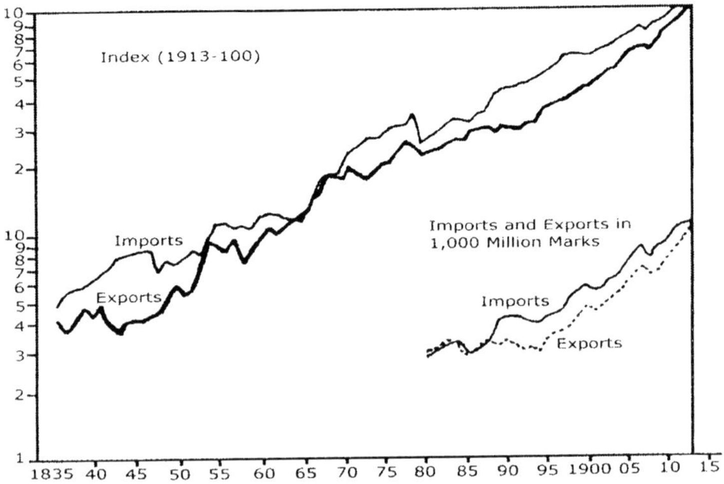

Source: Borchardt (1973), 114.

From the 1870s on, as Germany's foreign trade "industrialized" and Germany ceased to be a supplier of agricultural products to Britain, German success made Germany increasingly look like a challenger to Britain. This helps to explain the developing rivalry between the two.[3]

This experience created intensive public discussion during the 1880s. A royal commission investigated the "causes of the depression of trade and industry," and its report included, among other things, critical comments on the increasing sales of German products in British markets. Newspapers publicized the issue, and it led to the "Merchandise Mark Act" of 1887, which required non-British products to list their country of origin. This is the origin of the famous "Made in Germany" label. The purpose of the act was originally to discriminate against foreign products: in fact, though, the requirements ended up helping German sales in the U.K., for German goods were thought to be of superior quality.[4]

Growing Protectionism after 1870

In the last quarter of the nineteenth century the liberal international economic order weakened and began to give way to powerful protectionist tendencies, especially in Europe. Industrial exports were affected, of course, but the main driving force was agriculture. Since the 1870s, European agriculture came to fear the competition of American grain producers. Thanks to the fall in transportation costs, North American grain entered the European markets and prices fell. Agrarian protectionism was Europe's principal answer.

Protectionism was not Europe's only answer, however. Great Britain responded by letting its grain-producing sector shrink. In the thirty years between the 1870s and the 1900s wheat prices fell sharply, "real" wheat prices falling by more than 30 percent. Land prices and rents fell even more! This led to a shift of capital and labor out of agriculture.[5] This "liberal" economic answer to foreign

3. C. Buchheim, *Deutsche Gewerbeexporte nach England in der zweiten Hälfte des 19. Jahrhunderts* (Ostfildern, 1983).

4. S. Pollard, "'Made in Germany' – die Angst vor der deutschen Konkurrenz im spätviktorianischen England," *Technikgeschichte* 54 (1987): 183–95.

5. See on this K. O'Rourke, *The European Grain Invasion 1870–1913*, Working Paper Series, University of Dublin, Centre for Economic Research (Dublin, 1997).

competition had sociopolitical roots. British landowners, we must remember, were, numerically speaking, a tiny elite group, farms were mostly very large by European standards. A mass political movement favoring agricultural protection could not be built on such a basis. Free trade thus prevailed in Britain.

How different were Continental conditions! In Germany, France, in Italy, and elsewhere, hundreds of thousands of middle-class producers represented fertile soil for protectionist movements (as we have seen for Germany, e.g., in chapter 5). Parliaments responded; protective tariffs were a result; and, significantly, the fall of land prices and rents in such countries was arrested. That was a politically engineered brake on the redistribution of income away from landowners, one with negative consequences for consumers. Tariff policy, as we have seen, had social costs.

Great Britain, however, did react with a significant policy measure. Instead of protective tariffs, it opted for a strengthening of empire and a global defense policy, designed to protect the sea lanes of British trade, and particularly its imports of foodstuffs: symbolized in the Naval Defence Act of 1889.[6] Like Continental protectionism, this was also a reaction with social costs.

Outside of agriculture, protectionism had more diffuse effects. For low-cost German steel producers, for example, tariffs by the 1880s were basically redundant. They proved nevertheless useful by permitting cartels to work at home; and they also aided periodic dumping efforts.[7] In other sectors of industry tariffs may have encouraged foreign investment in Germany and brought technological change along with it, thus possibly counteracting the original intention of the tariffs. International cartels, in any case, were certainly one generalized European response to international competition and the national cartels it had engendered. By 1914 there were over 110 international associations and agreements, including nineteen in the chemical sector, eighteen in transportation, fifteen in textiles and twenty-six in coal, ores, metals—all with very different specific aims. Some agreements mainly controlled domestic markets, others affected export markets. In sum, cartels, like the tariffs, severely restricted international competition and hindered the further development of free markets.

---

6. See on this the penetrating analysis of A. Offer, *The First World War: An Agrarian Interpretation* (Oxford and New York, 1989).

7. On this, see Webb (1982), 309–26. See also chapter 6 on agrarian protectionism.

Foreign Investment

The second half of the nineteenth century was also an age of expanding international capital mobility. Indeed, by some standards, the degree of international mobility reached in the 1850–1914 era was not again equaled until very recently.[8] The principal form of capital exports then was portfolio investment—the purchase by investors of one country of the securities of governments and enterprises of another country. This foreign investment went largely into the development of resource-rich "countries of recent settlement," mainly by the financing of infrastructure projects (railways, port facilities, power plants, and so forth). Direct investment—often associated with the increasing numbers of multinational enterprises—also grew in the period. Graph 20 gives a rough idea of the growing relative importance of both forms of foreign investment for a number of leading capital exporters. This is a higher share than we find in most capital exporters today.

Graph 20: An Index of Capital Mobility: Current Account Surplus and Deficit as Percentage of GNP in Selected Countries and Years (1870–1910)

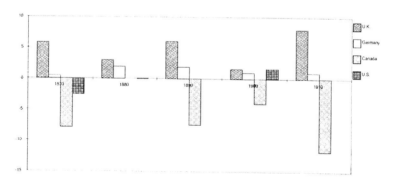

Source: R. Tilly, *Globalisierung aus historischer Sicht und das Lernen aus der Geschichte,* Kölner Vorträge zur Wirtschafts- und Sozialgeschichte 41 (Cologne, 1999), 24.

8. For an overview, see P. Bairoch and R. Kozul Wright, *Globalization Myths: Some Historical Reflections on Integration, Industrialization, and Growth in the World Economy,* United Nations Conference on Trade and Development. Discussion Paper No. 113 (March 1996); also R. Tilly, *Globalisierung aus historischer Sicht und das Lernen aus der Geschichte,* Kölner Vorträge zur Wirtschafts- und Sozialgeschichte 41 (Cologne, 1999).

Chronologically and quantitatively Great Britain led the world in nineteenth-century foreign investment. By the 1870s London had become the world's international financial center, and soon was to become the great market to which investors of other countries, e.g., Austria, Germany, or Italy, also channeled their capital.[9] France became the world's second largest capital exporter in this period. German foreign investment came later, and remained well behind that of Britain and France, since domestic economic development held capital at home. Nevertheless, by the eve of World War I, Germany had become a major source of foreign investment, mainly, but not solely, in Europe. Table 52 offers a comparative picture of the overall pattern for the leading investors and recipients of capital.

Table 52: Foreign Investment on the Eve of World War I (1913–1914)

Creditor	Bill. Dollars	Debtor	Bill. Dollars
Great Britain	18.0	Europe	12.0
France	9.0	U.S. and Canada	10.5
Germany	5.8	Latin America	8.5
U.S.	3.5	Asia	6.0
Belgium, Netherlands, Switzerland	5.5	Africa	4.7
Other countries	2.2	Australia	2.3
Total	44.0	Total	44.0

Source: Hardach (1977), 100.

We should not conclude this brief description without at least asking why or how this considerable foreign investment of the period could have come about. The proximate answer is that it was profitable. Capitalists invested in foreign countries because it paid to do so. For Germany we have some relevant estimates of the yields investors could expect to realize on the foreign securities they bought. One sees here the (slight) superiority of foreign securities traded in the Berlin market.[10] This is a result that is also observable in the London market in the same period.[11] Graph 21 compares domestic and foreign security returns in Berlin. Graph 22 then compares the overall returns in London and Berlin.

9. See L. Jenks, *The Migration of British Capital to 1875* (London, 1938); M. Edelstein, *Overseas Investment in the Age of High Imperialism* (London, 1982).
10. See R. Tilly, "Der deutsche Kapitalmarkt und die Auslandsinvestitionen von 1870 bis 1913," *Zeitschrift für empirische Wirtschaftsforschung* 2 (1992): 199–225.
11. On this, see Edelstein (1982).

Graph 21: Annual Yields on Domestic and Foreign Securities Traded in Berlin Capital Market (1870–1913)

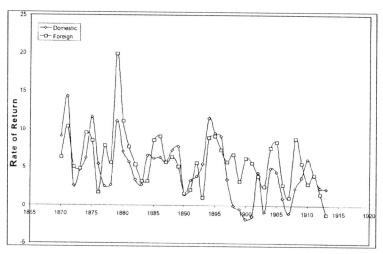

Source: Tilly (1999), 25.

Graph 22: Rates of Return on Securities Traded in Berlin and London Capital Markets (1871–1913)

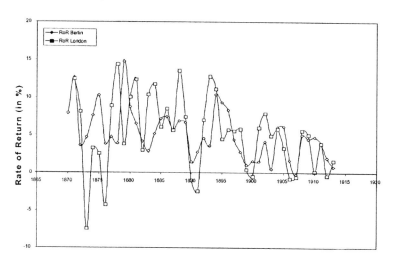

Source: Tilly (1999).

Note that yields in both markets decline as does the difference between the two markets. Note also that the gap between foreign and domestic yields in the Berlin market also diminishes (as it also did in the London market—a fact not shown here). We believe that these two tendencies—the diminishing differences between foreign and domestic yields and the declining yields themselves—reflected the increasing confidence of investors in foreign securities, their willingness to accept an ever smaller risk premium, as well as the growing integration of the international capital markets—one of the period's most striking features. The presumed perception of investors that the riskiness of foreign securities was declining was related, we believe, to the decreasing risk of currency depreciation. This, in turn, stemmed from the spread of the gold standard. Countries that adhered to the gold standard were perceived as accepting the gold standard rules, which meant a strong commitment to the maintenance of a sound, convertible currency, and investors could reward such a commitment by investing in the future of such countries. This widespread international consensus no doubt depended on a very particular political constellation, a kind of *Pax Britannica*, which came into being in the late nineteenth century, but which disintegrated in 1914. A comparable substitute first reappeared after 1945.

EPILOGUE

The year that marks the end of our history, 1914, is long ago. The German economy has undergone many changes since then. In very long-term perspective, it has prospered mightily. Living standards of Germany's population have increased by over 40 percent (in real terms)[1] since that fateful year. With a per capita income of nearly $20,000 per year, Germany is now one of the world's richest countries. In terms of leisure time and life expectancy, its relative position among the world's countries is still higher. That is well known.

Such a perspective, however, obscures many important parts of the picture of German economic history since 1914. Here is the place to discuss some of them, even if only briefly. The reason for so doing is to give ourselves a chance to step back and see the changes and achievements of Germany's nineteenth-century economic development in retrospect, but from our contemporary point of view. That is, we want to try to understand how much of the legacy of the nineteenth century has been modified by events of the twentieth. We turn, then, to the episodes of twentieth-century history which have shaped Germany since 1914.

First and foremost came World War I. It took a heavy direct toll in lives, material, and also in capital in the form of foregone investment. But by far the most drastic consequences were the political changes. On the domestic front, the young, democratic Weimar

---

1. See A. Ritschl and M. Spoerer, "Das Bruttosozialprodukt in Deutschland nach den amtlichen Volkseinkommens- und Sozialproduktstatistiken 1900–1995," *Jahrbuch für Wirtschaftsgeschichte* 2 (1997): 27–54. Since this index excludes new products not available in 1914, it is surely a lower-bound estimate of improvements in living standards over the twentieth century.

Republic was racked by distributional conflicts, especially between organized labor, on the one hand, and employers and capitalists, on the other. On the international front Weimar Germany's international relations were tainted by its forced acceptance of the Treaty of Versailles (1919), which brought a large reparations burden. Association with that treaty also discouraged the Weimar government from implementing policies that might have helped to restore external economic equilibrium, for such policies would have not only entailed downward pressure on wages and sacrifices from a population that had already suffered during the war, but would also have largely benefited—at least in the short turn—Germany's former enemies. The Great Inflation of 1919–23 followed from this unresolved situation. But even after the currency had been stabilized (in 1924) the new currency, the Reichsmark, remained a weak currency, Germany's external balance remained highly dependent on other countries' willingness to lend. The recovery of the mid 1920s, sometimes called "the golden twenties" was short-lived. The way to world economic collapse in the 1930s was not far.

The policy conflict between domestic and external stabilization persisted. In the last stages of the Weimar Republic, Reichschancellor Brüning's austerity measures—ostensibly aimed at the priority of restoring external equilibrium—succeeded only in exacerbating the unemployment problem at home and in alienating the majority of German voters. This failure, we now know, paved the way for the Nazi takeover in 1933 and Hitler's Third Reich. What followed is well known. Nazi policies restrained market forces, gradually closed the economy to external influences, and expanded domestic demand through government spending (mainly for military purposes). This is not the place to consider those policies in detail or to discuss how they were modified during World War II. Suffice it to say that they had an influence, possibly a long-run influence, on the structure and growth potential of the German economy, and also on the way economists, businessmen, and political leaders thought about it.

Summing up the interwar period in terms of our central theme, economic growth, one would have to say that the German economy performed poorly—well below its long-run potential. No doubt this had to do with national problems related to the structure of the economy and also to poor policies. Looking back at this segment of Germany's economic history, however, one cannot help but be struck by the crucial importance of its international relations. Compared with the pre-1914 years, the disintegration of the world economy in the 1920s and 1930s was surely the most significant change of all. Attempts at international cooperation collided time and time again with the reparations and war debts question.[2] This conflict was one of the decisive factors in the collapse of the world economy in the 1930s—and a major determinant of Germany's development since 1919. The key to the German economic malaise of the interwar years was thus both national and international.

If we then turn to the next chapter of German economic history—the post-1945 experience—we observe a radically altered grand scenario: the Cold War, two Germanys, and a series of U.S.-sponsored policy measures (such as the GATT, the Marshall Plan, or the EPU), which fostered international cooperation, integration, and reconstruction of the world economy, and which included the West German economy. Favored by this international constellation, that economy recovered at a remarkable rate. By the late 1950s, contemporaries were already speaking of Germany's "economic miracle." Even proponents of the so-called "reconstruction thesis"—according to which any reasonably sound economy would grow rapidly as it recovered from a shock such as war—acknowledged that the West German economy performed well, fully exploiting its long-run growth potential.[3]

Once again, the result can be attributed to national and international causes. First, it is said, West Germany prospered because international trade and payments restrictions were falling and because the countries with which Germany traded most were prospering and growing rapidly. Initial successes of the 1950s, associated with the Marshall Plan and the EPU, were assured continuity by the founding of the EEC in 1957, which made West Germany an integral part of Western Europe.[4] Second, many economists and

---

2. On this question, see B. Eichengreen, *Golden Fetters: The Gold Standard and the Great Depression, 1919–1939* (New York, 1992).

3. According to A. Maddison, *Monitoring the World Economy, 1820–1992,* Development Centre of the Organisation for Economic Cooperation and Development Paris, OECD Publications and Information Center (Washington, 1995), West Germany's per capita product grew more than twice as fast as that of the sixteen Western economies whose growth he has estimated (4.9 percent as compared to 2.3 percent per annum, 1950–73); L. Lindlar, *Das mißverstandene Wirtschaftswunder. Westdeutschland und die westeuropäische Nachkriegsprosperität* (Tübingen, 1997).

4. C. Buchheim, *Die Wiedereingliederung Westdeutschlands in die Weltwirtschaft 1945–1958* (Munich, 1990).

economic historians have stressed national causes; but they are divided on which national characteristic has been decisive. On the one hand, "Ordo-Liberal" reforms such as the currency and price reforms of 1948 freed the economy from dirigistic controls and laid the groundwork for the development of a strong, market economy. Here the emphasis is on competition and innovative entrepreneurs, and the new anti-cartel stance (Competition Law of 1957) is interpretable along these lines.[5] Many observers, on the other hand, see the same success as a result of the resurgence of Germany's traditional strengths: large-scale enterprises, working closely with large, universal banks, and cooperatively linked to one another through informal agreements on market-sharing and through cross-ownership ties, cooperating also with organized labor through the institution of codetermination. Some scholars have gone so far as to speak of a "German model" of "organized capitalism" as an explanation of German economic dynamism.[6] It has even been offered as a possible solution to the problems of many so-called emerging economies since the 1980s. Available evidence, in any case, can be mobilized to support both interpretations.

Such an assessment takes us back to the pre-1914 period. For one line of interpretation of Germany's successful industrialization stresses the syndrome of large-scale enterprises, great banks, cartels, other forms of cooperative enterprise, and also government support (e.g., through protective tariffs). This has been given the label "organized capitalism" (or "corporatist capitalism"). The international prominence of such heavy industries as steel, chemicals, and electrical engineering support this interpretation. An alternative school, however, stresses small-scale enterprises, concentrated in dynamic industrial regions, served by public transportation, educational and financial services, as the key to Germany's pre-1914 success. Here, the light engineering sector offers a case in point. According to this view, the "organized capitalism" syndrome was more a burden to be borne than a true national asset.

5. G. Ambrosius, *Die Durchsetzung der sozialen Marktwirtschaft in Westdeutschland 1945-1949* (Stuttgart, 1977).

6. One of the earliest to do so was A. Schonfield, *Modern Capitalism: The Changing Balance of Public and Private Power* (London, Oxford, and New York, 1969); see also V. Berghahn, *The Americanization of West German Industry, 1945-1973* (Leamington Spa and New York, 1986). For an interesting critique of this interpretation, see G. Herrigel, *Industrial Constructions: The Sources of German Industrial Power* (Cambridge, 1996).

It is our contention, however, that neither (or both) of these views is correct.[7] The German economy of the nineteenth century owed its success to its ability to adopt and further develop technologies that called for large amounts of capital and large-scale organizations; and it profited from cooperative institutions that helped to reduce uncertainty and risk. The relevant examples have already been mentioned. It is worth adding that these industries also supplied an important share of Germany's exports in the pre-1914 era. But German industrialization also built on its ability to produce a broad range of industrial goods, particularly those that embodied skilled labor (and education) and which were supplied by the country's thousands of small- and medium-sized enterprises (light engineering products, scientific instruments, optics, tools offer the best example). The State, operating at different levels, contributed to the development of both parts of the German economy. Today, it is still possible to see evidence of both parts at work. Today, however, the German economy is much more dependent on the world economy. It does not make much sense, we believe, to speak of a "German model" of development. The world economy was important for German development in the nineteenth century, but there was a greater role for indigenous economic and political institutions. Even then, however, the German economy was not monolithic.

7. Herrigel (1996), 1–27.

SELECTED BIBLIOGRAPHY

Abel, Wilhelm. *Der Pauperismus in Deutschland am Vorabend der industriellen Revolution.* Dortmund, 1966.
———. *Massenarmut und Hungerkrisen im vorindustriellen Europa.* Göttingen, 1986 [1977, 1972].
Abelshauser, Werner. "Umbruch und Persistenz. Das deutsche Produktionsregime in historischer Perspektive." In *Geschichte und Gesellschaft* 27 (2001): 503–23.
Albisetti, James C. *Secondary School Reform in Imperial Germany.* Princeton, 1983.
Ambrosius, Gerold. *Die Durchsetzung der sozialen Marktwirtschaft in Westdeutschland 1945–1949.* Stuttgart, 1977.
Aretin, Karl Otmar Freiherr von. *Das Reich. Friedensgarantie und europäisches Gleichgewicht, 1648–1806.* Stuttgart, 1986.
Bade, Klaus J. "Die deutsche überseeische Massenauswanderung im 19. und frühen 20. Jahrhundert. Bestimmungsfaktoren und Entwicklungsbedingungen." In idem, *Auswanderer – Wanderarbeiter – Gastarbeiter: Bevölkerung, Arbeitsmarkt und Wanderung in Deutschland in der Mitte des 19. Jahrhunderts,* 259–99. Vol. 1 (2 vols.). Ostfildern, 1984.
———. "Labor Migration and the State: Germany from the Late 19th Century to the Onset of the Great Depression." In *Population, Labor and Migration in 19th- and 20th-Century Germany,* edited by Klaus J. Bade, 59–85. German Historical Perspectives 1. Leamington Spa i.a., 1987.
Bairoch, Paul. "Agriculture and the Industrial Revolution." In *Fontana Economic History of Europe,* edited by Carlo M. Cipolla, 452–506. Vol. 3. (6 vols.). London, 1969.
———. *The Economic Development of the Third World Since 1900.* Berkeley, 1975.
Bairoch, Paul, and Richard Kozul Wright. "Globalization Myths: Some Historical Reflections on Integration, Industrialization, and Growth in the World Economy." *United Nations Conference on Trade and Development.* Discussion Paper No. 113 (March 1996).
Barkin, Kenneth D. *The Controversy over German Industrialization 1890–1902.* Chicago, 1970.

Berding, Helmut, ed. *Wirtschaftliche und politische Integration in Europa im 19. und 20. Jahrhundert.* Göttingen, 1984.

Berghahn, Volker. *The Americanization of West German Industry, 1945–1973.* Leamington Spa and New York, 1986.

Berghoff, Hartmut, and R. Moeller. "Tired Pioneers and Dynamic Newcomers? A Comparative Essay on English and German Entrepreneurial History, 1870–1914." *Economic History Review* 47 (1994): 262–87.

Bergmann, Jürgen. "Ökonomische Voraussetzungen der Revolution von 1848. Zur Krise von 1845–48 in Deutschland." In *Zweihundert Jahre amerikanische Revolution und moderne Revolutionsforschung,* edited by Hans-Ulrich Wehler, 254–87. Geschichte und Gesellschaft, Sonderheft 2. Göttingen, 1976.

Blackbourn, David, and Richard J. Evans, eds. *The German Bourgeoisie.* London, 1991.

Blumberg, Horst. "Die Finanzierung der Neugründungen und Erweiterungen von Industriebetrieben in Form der Aktiengesellschaften während der fünfziger Jahre des 19. Jahrhunderts in Deutschland, am Beispiel der preußischen Verhältnisse erläutert." In *Studien zur Geschichte der industriellen Revolution in Deutschland,* edited by Hans Mottek et al., 164–208. Berlin, 1960.

Böhme, Helmut. *Deutschlands Weg zur Großmacht. Studien zum Verhältnis von Wirtschaft und Staat während der Reichsgründungszeit 1848–1881.* Cologne, 1966.

Borchard, Karl. *Staatsverbrauch und öffentliche Investitionen in Deutschland 1780–1850.* Göttingen, 1968.

Borchardt, Knut. "The Industrial Revolution in Germany 1700–1914." In *Fontana Economic History of Europe,* edited by Carlo M. Cipolla, 76–160. Vol. 4.1 (6 vols.). London, 1973.

———. "Die Frage des Kapitalmangels in der ersten Hälfte des 19. Jahrhunderts in Deutschland." In *Wachstum, Krisen, Handlungsspielräume der Wirtschaftspolitik. Studien zur Wirtschaftsgeschichte des 19. und 20. Jahrhunderts,* 28–41. Kritische Studien zur Geschichtswissenschaft 50. Göttingen, 1982.

———. "Protektionismus im historischen Rueckblick." In *Der neue Protektionismus,* edited by Armin Gutowski, 17–47. Hamburgisches Welt-Wirtschafts-Archiv. Hamburg, 1984.

Bowden, Witt, Michael Karpovich, and Abbot P. Usher. *An Economic History of Europe Since 1750.* New York, 1937.

Brepohl, Wilhelm. *Der Aufbau des Ruhrvolkes im Zuge der Ost-West-Wanderung. Beiträge zur deutschen Sozialgeschichte des 19. und 20 Jahrhunderts.* Soziale Forschung und Praxis 7. Recklinghausen, 1948.

Brockhage, Bernhard. *Zur Entwicklung des preussisch-deutschen Kapitalexports.* Leipzig, 1910.

Brophy, James M. *Capitalism, Politics and Railroads in Prussia, 1830–1870.* Columbus, 1998.

Brose, Eric Dorn. *The Politics of Technological Change in Prussia: Out of the Shadow of Antiquity 1809–1848.* Princeton, 1993.

Brown, John. "Coping with Crisis? The Diffusion of Waterworks in Late Nineteenth Century German Towns." *Journal of Economic History* 48 (1988): 307–18.

Buchheim, Christoph. *Deutsche Gewerbeexporte nach England in der zweiten Hälfte des 19. Jahrhunderts.* Ostfildern, 1983.

———. *Die Wiedereingliederung Westdeutschlands in die Weltwirtschaft 1945–1958.* Munich, 1990.

———. *Industrielle Revolutionen. Langfristige Entwicklung in Großbritannien, Europa und Übersee.* Munich, 1994.

Carson, Carol. *The History of the United States National Income and Product Accounts: The Development of an Analytical Tool, Review of Income and Wealth.* New Haven, 1975.

Cerman, Markus, and Sheilagh Ogilvie, eds. *Protoindustrialisierung in Europa. Industrielle Revolution vor dem Fabrikzeitalter.* Historische Sozialkunde 5. Vienna, 1994.

Conze, Werner. "Vom Pöbel zum Proletariat. Sozialgeschichtliche Voraussetzungen für den Sozialismus in Deutschland." *Vierteljahrschrift für Sozial- und Wirtschaftsgeschichte* 41 (1954): 333–64.

Crafts, Nick F. R. "Gross National Product in Europe 1870–1910: Some New Estimates." *Explorations in Economic History* 20 (1983): 387–401.

———. "British Industrialization in an International Context" Journal of Interdisciplinary History 19 (1989): 415–28.

———. "Exogenous or Endogenous Growth? The Industrial Revolution Reconsidered." *Journal of Economic History* 55 (1995): 745–72.

Crouzet, François. "Wars, Blockade, and Economic Change in Europe, 1792–1815." *Journal of Economic History* 24 (1964): 567–88.

Dickler, Robert. "Organization and Change in Productivity in Eastern Prussia. Labour Market Pressure Aspects of Agricultural Growth in the Eastern Region of Prussia, 1840–1914: A Case Study of Economic Demographic Transition." Ph.D. diss., University of Pennsylvania, 1975.

———. "Organization and Change in Productivity." In *European Peasants and Their Markets*, edited by W. N. Parker and E. Jones. Princeton, 1975.

Dipper, Christof. *Die Bauernbefreiung in Deutschland 1780–1850.* Stuttgart, 1980.

———. *Deutsche Geschichte 1648–1789.* Frankfurt am Main, 1991.

Dumke, Rolf H. "The Political Economy of German Economic Unification: Tariffs, Trade and Politics of the Zollverein Era." Ph.D. diss. (unpublished), University of Wisconsin, 1976.

———. "Die wirtschaftlichen Folgen des Zollvereins." In *Deutsche Wirtschaftsgeschichte im Industriezeitalter. Konjunktur, Krise, Wachstum*, edited by Werner Abelshauser and Dietmar Petzina, 241–73 Düsseldorf, 1981.

———. "Der deutsche Zollverein als Modell ökonomischer Integration." In *Wirtschaft und politische Integration in Europa im 19. und 20. Jahrhundert*, edited by Helmut Berding, 71–101. Geschichte und Gesellschaft, Sonderheft 10. Göttingen, 1984.

Durchardt, Heinz. *Altes Reich und europäische Staatenwelt, 1648–1806.* Enzyklopädie Deutscher Geschichte 4, Munich, 1990.

———. *Das Zeitalter des Absolutismus.* Grundriß der Geschichte 11. Munich, 1992.

Edelmann, Heidrun. *Vom Luxusgut zum Gebrauchsgegenstand. Die Geschichte der Verbreitung von Personenkraftwagen in Deutschland.* Frankfurt am Main, 1989.

Edelstein, Michael. *Overseas Investment in the Age of High Imperialism: The United Kingdom, 1850 to 1914.* London, 1982.

Eichengreen, Barry J. *Golden Fetters: The Gold Standard and the Great Depression, 1919–1939.* New York, 1992.

Eichholtz, Dietrich. *Junker und Bourgeoisie vor 1848 in der preußischen Eisenbahngeschichte*. Berlin, 1962.

Engel, Ernst. *Das Zeitalter des Dampfes in technisch-statistischer Beleuchtung*. Berlin, 1879.

Erickson, Charlotte. *British Industrialists: Steel and Hosiery, 1850–1950*. National Institute of Economic and Social Research. Economic and Social Studies 18. Cambridge, 1959.

Fehrenbach, Elisabeth. *Vom Ancien Regime zum Wiener Kongress*. Grundriß der Geschichte 12. Munich, 1981.

————. *Verfassungsstaat und Nationenbildung, 1815–1871*. Enzyklopädie Deutscher Geschichte 22. Munich, 1992.

Feldenkirchen, Wilfried. "Banking and Economic Growth: Banks and Industry in Germany in the Nineteenth Century and Their Changing Relationship During Industrialisation." In *German Industry and German Industrialisation*, edited by William Robert Lee, 116–47. London, 1991.

Fischer, Wolfram. "German Zollverein: A Case Study in Customs Union." *Kyklos* 13 (1960): 65–89.

————. "Die Stellung der preußischen Bergrechtreform von 1851–1865 in der Wirtschafts- und Sozialverfassung des 19. Jahrhunderts." Reprinted in idem, *Wirtschaft und Gesellschaft im Zeitalter der Industrialisierung. Aufsätze – Studien – Verträge*, 148–60. Göttingen, 1972.

————. *Die Weltwirtschaft im 20. Jahrhundert*. Göttingen, 1979.

————. *Expansion, Integration, Globalisierung*. Göttingen, 1998.

Fischer, Wolfram, Jochen Krengel, and Jutta Wietog. *Sozialgeschichtliches Arbeitsbuch*. Vol. 1, *Materialien zur Statistik des Deutschen Bundes (1815–1870)*. Munich, 1982.

Filk, Rainer. "Motorisierung und Automobilindustrie in Deutschland bis 1933." Habilitation thesis, Eichstätt, 1999.

Floud, Roderick, and Donald McClosekey, eds. *The Economic History of Modern Britain*. Cambridge, 1994.

Franz, Günther. "Landwirtschaft 1800–1850. " In *Handbuch der deutschen Wirtschafts- und Sozialgeschichte*, edited by Hermann Aubin and Wolfgang Zorn, 276–320. Vol. 2 (2 vols.). Stuttgart, 1976.

Fremdling, Rainer. *Eisenbahnen und deutsches Wirtschaftswachstum 1840–1879*. Dortmund, 1975.

————. "Railroads and German Economic Growth: A Leading Sector Analysis with a Comparison to the United States and Great Britain." *Journal of Economic History* 37 (1977): 583–604.

————. "Modernisierung und Wachstum der Schwerindustrie in Deutschland, 1830–1860." *Geschichte und Gesellschaft* 5 (1979): 201–27.

————. "Freight Rates and State Budget: The Role of the National Prussian Railways, 1880–1913. " *Journal of European Economic History* 9 (1980): 21–39.

————. "Die Rolle ausländischer Facharbeiter bei der Einführung neuer Techniken im Deutschland des 19. Jahrhunderts (Textilindustrie, Maschinenbau, Schwerindustrie)." *Archiv für Sozialgeschichte* 24 (1984): 1–45.

————. *Technologischer Wandel und Internationaler Handel im 18. und 19. Jahrhundert*. Berlin, 1986.

———. "Foreign Competition and Technological Change: British Exports and the Modernization of German Iron Industry from the 1820s to the 1860s." In *German Industry and German Industrialization: Essays in German Economic and Business History in the Nineteenth and Twentieth Centuries*, edited by William Robert Lee, 47–76. London, 1991.

Gerschenkron, Alexander. *Bread and Democracy in Germany.* Berkeley, 1943.

———. *Economic Backwardness in Historical Perspective.* Cambridge, 1962.

Günther, Franz. "Landwirtschaft 1800–1850." In *Handbuch der deutschen Wirtschafts- und Sozialgeschichte*, edited by Hermann Aubin and Wolfgang Zorn. Vol. 2. Stuttgart, 1976.

Hahn, Hans-Werner. *Geschichte des Deutschen Zollvereins.* Göttingen, 1984.

———. "Hegemonie und Integration. Vorraussetzungen und Folgen der preußischen Führungsrolle im Deutschen Zollverein." In *Wirtschaftliche und politische Integration in Europa im 19. und 20. Jahrhundert*, edited by Helmut Berding, 45–70. Geschichte und Gesellschaft, Sonderheft 10. Göttingen, 1984.

Hardach, Gerd. *Die Bedeutung wirtschaftlicher Faktoren bei der Wiedereinführung der Eisen- und Getreidezölle in Deutschland 1879.* Berlin, 1967.

———. *Deutschland in der Weltwirtschaft 1870–1970.* Frankfurt am Main, 1977.

Harnisch, Hartmut. *Kapitalistische Agrarreformen und industrielle Revolution. Agrarhistorische Untersuchungen über das ostelbische Preußen zwischen Spätfeudalismus und bürgerlich-demokratischer Revolution von 1848/49 unter besonderer Berücksichtigung der Provinz Brandenburg.* Weimar, 1984.

———. "Georg Friedrich Knapp. Agrargeschichtsforschung und sozialpolitisches Engagement im Deutschen Kaiserreich." *Jahrbuch für Wirtschaftsgeschichte* 1 (1993): 95–132.

Helling, Gertrud. "Zur Entwicklung der Produktivität in der deutschen Landwirtschaft im 19. Jahrhundert." *Jahrbuch für Wirtschaftsgeschichte* 1 (1966): 129–41.

Henderson, William Otto. *The State and the Industrial Revolution in Prussia 1740–1870.* Liverpool, 1958.

———. *The Industrial Revolution on the Continent: Germany, France, Russia 1800–1914.* London, 1967.

———. *The Zollverein.* Cambridge, 1939; London, 1968 [1959].

Henning, Friedrich Wilhelm. "Die Betriebsgrößenstruktur der mitteleuropäischen Landwirtschaft im 18. Jahrhundert und ihr Einfluß auf die ländlichen Einkommensverhältnisse." *Zeitschrift für Agrargeschichte und Agrarsoziologie* 17 (1969): 171–93.

———. *Das vorindustrielle Deutschland 800–1800.* Wirtschafts- und Sozialgeschichte 1. Paderborn, 1994.

Herrigel, Gary. *Industrial Constructions: The Sources of German Industrial Power.* Cambridge, 1996.

Hilferding, Rudolf. *Das Finanzkapital.* Berlin, 1909.

Hoffmann, Walther G. *Das Wachstum der deutschen Wirtschaft seit der Mitte des 19. Jahrhunderts.* Berlin/Heidelberg/New York, 1965.

———. "The Take-Off in Germany." In *The Economics of Take-Off into Sustained Growth*, edited by Walt Whitman Rostow, 95–118. London, 1969.

Hoffmann, Walther G., and J. Müller. *Das deutsche Volkseinkommen, 1851–1957.* Tübingen, 1959.

Hohorst, Gerd, Jürgen Kocka, and Gerhard A. Ritter. *Sozialgeschichtliches Arbeits-buch.* Vol. 2, *Materialien zur Statistik des Kaiserreiches (1870–1914).* Munich, 1978 [1975].

Holtfrerich, Carl-Ludwig. "Quantitative Wirtschaftsgeschichte des Ruhrkohlen-bergbaus im 19. Jahrhundert. Eine Führungssektoranalyse." Ph.D. diss., University of Münster, 1971, and University of Dortmund, 1973.

———. "The Monetary Unification Process in Nineteenth-Century Germany: Relevance and Lessons for Europe Today." In *A European Central Bank? Per-spectives on Monetary Unification after Ten Years of the EMS,* edited by Marcello de Cecco and Alberto Giovannini, 216–41. Cambridge, 1989.

Hühner, Michael. "Kommunalfinanzen, Kommunalunternehmen und Kommunal-politik im Deutschen Kaiserreich." Münsteraner Beiträge zur Cliometrie und quantitativen Wirtschaftsgeschichte 6. Ph.D. diss., University of Münster, 1998.

Jaeger, Hans. *Unternehmer in der deutschen Politik (1890–1918).* Bonn, 1967.

Jantke, Carl. "Zur Deutung des Pauperismus." In *Die Eigentumslosen. Der deutsche Pauperismus und die Emanzipationskrise in Darstellungen und Deutungen der zeitgenössischen Literatur,* edited by Dietrich Hilger and Carl Jantke, 7–47. Munich, 1965.

Jarausch, Konrad Hugo. *Students, Society and Politics in Imperial Germany.* Prince-ton, 1982.

Jenks, Leland. *The Migration of British Capital to 1875.* London, 1938.

Kaelble, Hartmut. *Industrielle Interessenpolitik in der Wilhelminischen Gesellschaft. Centralverband Deutscher Industrieller, 1895–1914.* Berlin, 1967.

———. *Berliner Unternehmer während der frühen Industrialisierung.* Berlin, 1972.

———. *Soziale Mobilität und Chancengleichheit im 19. und 20. Jahrhundert.* Göttingen, 1983.

Kamphoefner, Walter. *Westfalen in der neuen Welt: eine Sozialgeschichte der Auswan-derung im 19. Jahrhundert.* Münster, 1982.

———. *The Westfalians: From Germany to Missouri.* Princeton, 1987.

Kehr, Eckart. *Der Primat der Innenpolitik.* Berlin, 1965.

Kell, Eva. *Das Fürstentum Leiningen. Umbruchserfahrungen einer Adelsherrschaft zur Zeit der Französischen Revolution.* Kaiserslautern, 1993.

Klessmann, Christoph. "Long-Distance Migration. Integration and Segregation of an Ethnic Minority in Industrial Germany: The Case of the Ruhr Poles." In *Pop-ulation, Labor and Migration in 19th- and 20th-Century Germany,* edited by Klaus J. Bade, 101–14. German Historical Perspectives 1. Leamington Spa i.a., 1987.

Knapp, Georg F. *Die Bauernbefreiung und der Ursprung der Landarbeiter in den älteren Theilen Preußens.* 2 Vols. Munich, 1887.

Knodel, John. *The Decline of Fertility in Germany, 1871–1939.* Princeton, 1976.

———. *Demographic Behavior in the Past.* Cambridge, 1988.

Kocka, Jürgen. *Unternehmensverwaltung und Angestelltenschaft am Beispiel Siemens, 1847–1914.* Stuttgart, 1969.

———. *Unternehmer in der deutschen Industrialisierung.* Göttingen, 1975.

———. *Weder Stand noch Klasse, Unterschichten um 1800.* Bonn, 1990.

Köllmann, Wolfgang. *Bevölkerung in der industriellen Revolution.* Göttingen, 1974.

———. "Bevölkerung und Arbeitskräftepotential in Deutschland, 1815–1870." Reprinted in idem, *Bevölkerung in der industriellen Revolution,* 61–98. Göttin-gen, 1974.

———. "Industrialisierung, Binnenwanderung und 'soziale Frage.'" Reprinted in idem, *Bevölkerung in der industriellen Revolution*, 106–24. Göttingen, 1974.

Komlos, John. *Nutrition and Economic Development in the Eighteenth-Century Habsburg Monarchy: An Anthropometric History*. Princeton, 1989.

———. "Ein Überblick über die Konzeptionen der Industriellen Revolution." *Vierteljahrschrift für Sozial- und Wirtschaftsgeschichte* 84 (1997): 461–511.

———. "The New World's Contribution to Food Consumption during the Industrial Revolution." *Journal of European Economic History* 27 (1998): 67–82.

Königlich Preussisches Statistisches Büro. *Preussische Statistik*. Vol. 4. Berlin, 1864.

Kopsidis, Michael. *Marktintegration und Entwicklung der westfälischen Landwirtschaft 1780–1880. Marktorientierte ökonomische Entwicklung eines bäuerlich strukturierten Agrarsektors*. Münster, 1996.

Krabbe, Wolfgang. *Kommunalpolitik und Industrialisierung*. Stuttgart, 1985.

Kriedte, Peter, Hans Medick, and Jürgen Schlumbohm. *Industrialisierung vor der Industrialisierung. Gewerbliche Warenproduktion auf dem Land in der Formationsphase des Kapitalismus*. Göttingen, 1978.

Kubitschek, Helmut. "Die Börsenverordnung von 28. Mai 1844 und die Situation im Finanz- und Kreditwesen Preußens in den vierziger Jahren des 19. Jahrhunderts (1840 bis 1847)." *Jahrbuch für Wirtschaftsgeschichte* 4 (1962): 57–78.

Kuczynski, Jürgen. *Geschichte der Lage der Arbeiter unter dem Kapitalismus*. Vol. 1, *Darstellung der Lage der Arbeiter in Deutschland von 1789 bis 1849*. 38 vols. Berlin, 1961.

Kuznets, Simon. *National Income and Its Composition 1919–1933*. 2 vols. New York, 1941.

Kwack, Tae-Yal. "Die Entwicklung von Kommunalunternehmen in Deutschland im 19. und frühen Jahrhundert – unter besonderer Berücksichtigung finanz- und sozialpolitischer Aspekte." Ph.D. diss., University of Münster, 1989.

Laer, Hermann von. *Industrialisierung und Qualität der Arbeit. Eine bildungsökonomische Untersuchung für das 19. Jahrhundert*. New York, 1977.

Landes, David S. *The Unbound Prometheus*. Cambridge, 1969.

Lee, Joseph J. "Labor in German Industrialization." In *Cambridge Economic History of Europe*, edited by Peter Mathias and M. M. Postan, 442–91. Vol. 7.1 (8 vols.). Cambridge, 1978.

Lee, William Robert. "Germany." In *European Demography and Economic Growth*, edited by William Robert Lee, 144–95. London, 1979.

———. "Economic Development and the State in the Nineteenth Century in Germany." *Economic History Review* 41 (1988): 346–67.

Lévy-Leboyer, Maurice, and François Bourguigon. *The French Economy in the Nineteenth Century*. Cambridge, 1990.

Lewis, W. Arthur. "Economic Development with Unlimited Supplies of Labour." *The Manchester School* 22 (1954): 139–91.

Lindlar, Ludger. *Das mißverstandene Wirtschaftswunder. Westdeutschland und die westeuropäische Nachkriegsprosperität*. Tübingen, 1997.

Maddison, Angus. *Monitoring the World Economy, 1820–1992*. Development Centre of the Organisation for Economic Cooperation and Development Paris, OECD Publications and Information Center. Washington, 1995.

Marquardt, Frederick. "Pauperism in Germany during the Vormärz. " *Central European Review* 2 (1969): 77–88.

Marschalck, Peter. *Deutsche Überseewanderungen im 19. Jahrhundert. Ein Beitrag zur soziologischen Theorie der Bevölkerung.* Stuttgart, 1973.

——. *Bevölkerungsgeschichte Deutschlands im 19. und 20. Jahrhundert.* Frankfurt am Main, 1984.

McCelland, Charles E. *State, Society and University in Germany 1700–1940.* Cambridge, 1980.

McClelland, David. *The Achieving Society.* Toronto, 1961.

Mendels, Franklyn. "Proto-industrialization: The First Phase of the Industrialization Process." *Journal of Economic History* 32 (1972): 241–61.

Milward, Alan S., and S. B. Saul. *The Economic Development of Continental Europe 1780–1870.* London, 1973.

Neuburger, Hugh M. *German Banks and German Economic Growth from Unification to World War I.* New York, 1977.

Neuburger, Hugh M., and Houston H. Stokes. "German Banks and German Growth, 1883–1913: An Empirical View." *Journal of Economic History* 34 (1974): 710–31.

——. "German Banks and German Growth: Reply." *Journal of Economic History* 36 (1976): 425–27.

O'Brien, Patrick, and Caglar Keyder. *Economic Growth in Britain and France 1780–1914.* London, 1978.

Offer, Avner. *The First World War: An Agrarian Interpretation.* Oxford and New York, 1989.

Ohnishi, Takeo. "Zolltarifpolitik Preußens bis zur Gründung des deutschen Zollvereins. Ein Beitrag zur Finanz- und Außenpolitik Preußens." Ph.D. diss., University of Göttingen, 1973.

O'Rourke, Kevin. "The European Grain Invasion 1870–1913." Working Paper Series, University of Dublin, Centre for Economic Research. Dublin, 1997.

Parker, William N., and Eric Jones, eds. *European Peasants and Their Markets: Essays in Agrarian Change.* Princeton, 1975.

Perkins, John A. "The Agricultural Revolution in Germany, 1850–1914." *Journal of European Economic History* 10 (1981): 71–118.

Pierenkemper, Toni. *Die westfälischen Schwerindustriellen 1852–1913. Soziale Struktur und unternehmerischer Erfolg.* Göttingen, 1979.

——. *Arbeitsmarkt und Angestellte im deutschen Kaiserreich, 1880–1913. Interessen und Strategien als Elemente der Integration eines segmentierten Arbeitsmarktes.* Stuttgart, 1987.

——. "The Standard of Living and Employment in Germany 1850–1980: An Overview." *Journal of European Economic History* 16 (1987): 51–73.

——. "Der Agrarsektor im Entwicklungsprozeß. Einige theoretische Vorüberlegungen." In *Landwirtschaft und industrielle Entwicklung. Zur ökonomischen Bedeutung von Bauernbefreiung, Agrarreform und Agrarrevolution.* Stuttgart, 1989.

——. "Der Agrarsektor in der vorindustriellen Gesellschaft. Einige Anmerkungen zur preußischen Entwicklung 1815–1830 aus produktionstheoretischer Sicht." *Zeitschrift für Agrargeschichte und Agrarsoziologie* 37 (1989): 168–86.

——. *Unternehmensgeschichte. Eine Einführung in ihre Methoden und Ergebnisse.* Stuttgart, 2000.

Pollard, Sidney. *Peaceful Conquest: The Industrialization of Europe, 1760–1970.* Oxford, 1981.

———. "'Made in Germany' – die Angst vor der deutschen Konkurrenz im spätviktorianischen England." *Technikgeschichte* 54 (1987): 183–95.

Puhle, Hans-Jürgen. "Parlament, Parteien und Interssenverbände, 1890–1918." In *Das kaiserliche Deutschland. Politik und Gesellschaft, 1870–1918*, edited by Michael Stürmer. Düsseldorf, 1970.

Radtke, Wolfgang. *Die Preußische Seehandlung zwischen Staat und Wirtschaft in der Frühphase der Industrialisierung*. Berlin, 1981.

Reich, Norbert. "Auswirkungen der deutschen Aktienrechtsreform von 1884 auf die Konzentration der deutschen Wirtschaft." In *Recht und Entwicklung der Großunternehmen im 19. und frühen 20. Jahrhundert*, edited by Norbert Horn and Jürgen Kocka, 255–73. Kritische Studien zur Geschichtswissenschaft 40 Göttingen, 1979.

Reulecke, Jürgen. *Geschichte der Urbanisierung in Deutschland*. Frankfurt am Main, 1985.

Riesser, Jacob. *The German Great Banks and Their Concentration in Relation to the Economic Development of Germany*. Documentation of the U.S. National Monetary Commission. Washington, D.C., 1911.

Ringer, Fritz K. *The Decline of the German Mandarins: The German Academic Community, 1890–1933*. Cambridge, 1969.

Ritschl, Albrecht, and Mark Spoerer. "Das Bruttosozialprodukt in Deutschland nach den amtlichen Wolkseinkommens- und Sozialproduktsstatistiken 1901–1995." *Jahrbuch für Wirtschaftsgeschichte* 2 (1997): 27–54.

Ritter, Ulrich P. *Die Rolle des Staates in den Frühstadien der Industrialisierung. Die preußische Industrieförderung in der ersten Hälfte des 19. Jahrhunderts*. Berlin, 1961.

Rosenberg, Hans. *Die Weltwirtschaftskrise 1857–59*. Göttingen, 1974.

Rostow, Walt Whitman. *Stages of Economic Growth: A Non-Communist Manifesto*. Cambridge, 1960.

Schissler, Hanna. *Preußische Agrargesellschaft im Wandel*. Göttingen, 1978.

Schonfield, Andrew. *Modern Capitalism: The Changing Balance of Public and Private Power*. London/Oxford/New York, 1969.

Spree, Reinhard. *Die Wachstumszyklen der deutschen Wirtschaft von 1840 bis 1880*. Schriften zur Wirtschafts- und Sozialgeschichte 29. Berlin, 1977.

———. *Soziale Ungleichheit vor Krankheit und Tod*. Göttingen, 1981.

Sylla, Richard, and Gianni Toniolo, eds. *Patterns of European Industrialization: The Nineteenth Century*. London, 1991.

Tessner, Magnus. *Die deutsche Automobilindustrie im Strukturwandel 1919 bis 1938*. Cologne, 1994.

Teuteberg, Hans Jürgen. *Die deutsche Landwirtschaft beim Eintritt in die Phase der Hochindustrialisierung*. Cologne, 1977.

Thoma, Ralf. *Der Industriekomplex von A. Borsig. Unternehmensentwicklung von 1837 bis 1932 und betriebswirtschaftliche Analyse unter besonderer Berücksichtigung des oberschlesischen Borsigwerks*. Cologne, 2002.

Tilly, Richard. "Los von England. Probleme des Nationalismus in der deutschen Wirtschaftsgeschichte." *Zeitschrift für die gesamte Staatswissenschaft* 124 (1968): 179–96.

———. "Capital Formation in Germany." In *Cambridge Economic History of Europe*, edited by Mathias Peter. Cambridge, 1978.

———. "Banken und Industrialisierung in Deutschland: Quantifizierungsversuche." In *Entwicklung und Aufgaben von Versicherungen und Banken in der Industrialisierung,* edited by Friedrich-Wilhelm Henning, 165–93. Schriften des Vereins für Socialpolitik, Neue Folge 105. Berlin, 1980.

———. "Mergers, External Growth and Finance in the Development of Large-Scale Enterprises in Germany, 1880–1913." *Journal of Economic History* 42 (1982): 629–58.

———. "German Banking, 1850–1914. Development Assistance for the Strong." *Journal of European Economic History* 15 (1986): 113–52.

———. *Vom Zollverein zum Industriestaat. Die wirtschaftlich-soziale Entwicklung Deutschlands 1834 bis 1914.* Munich, 1990.

———. "An Overview on the Role of the Large German Banks up to 1914." In *Finance and Financiers in European History, 1880–1960,* edited by Youssif Cassis, 93–112. Cambridge, 1992.

———. "Der deutsche Kapitalmarkt und die Auslandsinvestitionen von 1870 bis 1913." *IFO-Studien. Zeitschrift für empirische Wirtschaftsforschung* 38, no. 2 (1992): 199–225.

———. "'Perestroika á la Prusse'. Preussens liberale Reformen zu Anfang des 19. Jahrhunderts im Lichte des Transformationsparadigmas." *Jahrbuch für Wirtschaftsgeschichte* 2 (1996): 147–60.

———. "Städtewachstum, Kommunalfinanzen und Munizipalsozialismus in der deutschen Industrialisierung. Eine vergleichende Perspektive 1870–1913." In *Die Stadt als Dienstleistungszentrum. Beiträge zur Geschichte der Sozialstadt in Deutschland im 19. und frühen 20. Jahrhundert,* edited by Jürgen Reulecke, 125–52. St. Katharinen, 1995.

———. *Globalisierung aus historischer Sicht und das Lernen aus der Geschichte.* Kölner Vorträge zur Wirtschafts- und Sozialgeschichte 41. Cologne, 1999.

———. "Universal Banking in Historical Perspective." *Journal for Institutional Theoretical Economics* 154 (1998): 7–32.

Tipton, Frank B. *Regional Variations in the Economic Development of Germany during the Nineteenth Century.* Middletown, Conn., 1976.

Trebilcock, Clive. "Germany." In idem, *The Industrialization of the Continental Powers, 1780–1914,* 22–111. London, 1981.

Treitschke, Heinrich von. *Deutsche Geschichte im 19. Jahrhundert.* Leipzig, 1908.

Treue, Wilhelm. *Wirtschaftszustände und Wirtschaftspolitik in Preußen 1815–1825.* Stuttgart, 1937.

Ulmann, Hans-Peter. *Der Bund der Industriellen. Organisation, Einfluß und Politik klein- und mittelbetrieblicher Industrieller im Deutschen Kaiserreich, 1895–1914.* Göttingen, 1976.

Viebahn, Georg von. *Statistik des nördlichen und zollvereinten Deutschlands.* Berlin, 1862.

Wagenführ, Rolf. *Die Industriewirtschaft Entwicklungstendenzen der deutschen und internationalen Industrieproduktion 1860 bis 1932.* Vierteljahreshefte zur Konjunkturforschung, Sonderheft 31. Berlin, 1933.

Wagner, Adolf. *Agrar- und Industriestaat. Eine Auseinandersetzung mit den Nationalsozialen und mit Prof. L. Brentano über die Kehrseite des Industriestaates und zur Rechtfertigung agrarischen Zollschutzes.* Jena, 1901.

Webb, Steven B. "Agricultural Protection in Wilhelmine Germany: Forging an Empire with Pork and Rye." *Journal of Economic History* 42 (1982): 309–26.

————. "Tariffs, Cartels, Technology, and Growth in the German Steel Industry, 1870 to 1914." In *Selected Cliometric Studies on German Economic History*, edited by John Komlos, 45–65. Stuttgart, 1997.

Weber-Kellermann, Ingeborg. *Landleben im 19. Jahrhundert*. Munich, 1987.

Wehler, Hans-Ulrich. *Das Deutsche Kaiserreich 1871–1918*. Deutsche Geschichte 9. Göttingen, 1973.

————. *Deutsche Gesellschaftsgeschichte*. Vol. 1 (3 vols.). Munich, 1995 [1987].

Wellenreuther, Thomas. "Die Infragestellung des ökonomischen Liberalismus in Deutschland von ca. 1870 bis 1913." In *Geschichte der Wirtschaftspolitik*, edited by Richard Tilly. Munich and Vienna, 1993.

Wellhöner, Volker. *Großbanken und Großindustrie im Kaiserreich*. Kritische Studien zur Geschichtswissenschaft 85. Göttingen, 1989.

Wengenroth, Ulrich. "Unternehmensstrategien in Deutschland, England und Frankreich vor dem Ersten Weltkrieg." In *Die Eisen- und Stahlindustrie im Dortmunder Raum. Wirtschaftliche Entwicklung, soziale Strukturen und technologischer Wandel im 19. und 20. Jahrhundert*, edited by Ottfried Dascher, 305–20. Hagen, 1992.

Wetzel, Christoph. *Die Auswirkungen des Reichsbörsengesetzes von 1896 auf die Effektenbörsen im Deutschen Reich, insbesondere auf die Berliner Fondsbörse*. Münster, 1996.

Wiener, Martin J. *English Culture and the Decline of the Industrial Spirit, 1850–1980*. Cambridge, 1981.

Williamson, Jeffrey G. "The Evolution of Global Markets Since 1830: Background Evidence and Hypotheses." *Explorations in Economic History* 32 (1995): 141–96.

Williamson, Oliver. *The Economic Institutions of Capitalism*. New York, 1985.

Winkler, Heinrich August, ed. *Organisierter Kapitalismus. Voraussetzungen und Anfänge*. Göttingen, 1974.

Wischermann, Clemens. "Der Property-Rights-Ansatz und die 'neue' Wirtschaftsgeschichte." *Geschichte und Gesellschaft* 19 (1993): 239–58.

Witt, Peter-Christian. *Die Finanzpolitik des Deutschen Reiches, 1903–1913*. Lübeck, 1970.

Ziegler, Dieter. *Eisenbahnen und Staat im Zeitalter der Industrialisierung. Die Eisenbahnpolitik der deutschen Staaten im Vergleich*. Stuttgart, 1996.

INDEX

accident insurance law, 142
agrarian protection, 84
agrarian reforms, 23–24, 26–27, 49, 69
agricultural chemistry, 78
agricultural improvements, 75, 79–80
agricultural labor, 46–47, 49–50, 98, 101
agricultural population, 49–50, 87
agricultural production, 75–76, 78–79, 84, 87, 91
agricultural revolution, 75, 79
agricultural sector, 53, 76, 80–81, 86
agricultural workers, 45, 53, 78–79, 98
agriculture, xvi, 13, 15, 18, 21, 27–28, 30, 43–44, 46–47, 53–55, 75–85, 95, 103, 148, 151–152
Allgemeines Handelsgesetz, 137
Alsace-Lorraine railways, 139
apprenticeship system, 106
assembly line, 54

Bank of Prussia, 37, 114
banking, xvi, 37, 39, 64, 70, 113–119, 121, 124
bar iron, 55–57
Bildungsbürgertum, 128

birth rate, 92
Bismarck, Otto von, 11, 81, 93, 112, 139–143

Camphausen, Ludolf von, 132
capital, 18, 21–22, 29, 38–40, 42–45, 55, 58, 60-61, 64–65, 71, 76–77, 95, 105, 113, 118, 120, 122–124, 137, 145, 148, 151, 153–157, 161
capital allocation, 120
capital exports, 45, 153
capital formation, 29, 42–44
capital mobility, 153
Centralverband Deutscher Industrieller, 134
civil servants, 31–32, 126, 128, 143–144
coal industry, 67
coal trade, 66–67
Confederation of the Rhine, 4
Congress of Vienna, 7, 31
consumption, 13, 54, 56, 60, 63, 66, 78, 84, 87, 144
customs duties, 112

death rate, 91
demographic history, 90–91
demographic indices, 93
demographic transition, 90–91, 93, 95

demography, 87–88, 92
disability pensions, 142
domestic consumption, 84
Dresden Coinage Convention, 35

East Elbia, 25, 29, 98, 101
economic liberalism, 69, 136–137,
    139, 141
educational qualifications, 125,
    129
educational system, 107, 148
electrotechnical industry, 118
emigration, 89, 95, 97–98
employment, 14, 18, 28, 30, 46,
    49–52, 60, 64, 75, 92, 94–96,
    103–105, 107
Engels, Friedrich, 43
entrepreneurship, xvi, 123–125,
    127–134, 136
estate system, 25
European trade, 149
export structure, 57, 148
export-regions, 149

Federal Unemployment Office,
    112
fiscal policy, 140
foreign investment, 145, 152–154
foreign trade, 33, 137, 145, 149–151
forward linkages, 58, 65–66
free trade, 25, 32, 152
free-trade era, 146

German coinage union, 37
German Confederation, 7–11, 37
German customs union, 23
German emigration, 95, 97–98
German Empire, 3, 5, 11, 82, 146
German monetary and banking
    system, 37
German monetary integration, 23
German special path (Sonderweg),
    125
gold standard, 36–37, 146–147,
    156, 159

golden twenties, the, 158
Great Inflation, 158
Gründerboom, 117

Hansemann, Adolf von, 132
Health Insurance Law, 142
healthcare system, 110
heavy industry, 17, 21, 58–59, 81,
    113, 117, 120, 125, 139
Holy Roman Empire of the Ger-
    man Nation, 3–5, 7

immigration, 98, 100–101
import substitution, 61, 67, 80, 105
industrial improvements, 79–80
industrial investment, 18, 43–45,
    59
industrial laborers, 98
infant mortality, 91–92
infrastructure investment, 43
insurance, 93, 98, 115, 121, 137,
    139, 142–143
internal migration, 94, 101
international migration, 94
interwar period, 158
investment, 18–22, 30, 38–39,
    43–45, 59–63, 65–66, 70–71, 75,
    105, 113, 120–121, 140, 144–145,
    152–154, 157
investment rates, 44

Junker, 24n. 1, 139

Kaiserreich, 3, 11–12, 30, 105, 114,
    131, 138–139, 144

labor, 13–14, 18, 24–25, 28–29, 42,
    45–47, 49–53, 61, 69, 75–76,
    78–79, 81, 87, 89–95, 97–105,
    107, 109–112, 115, 124, 132,
    137–139, 142, 145, 151, 158,
    160–161
labor force, 13, 45–47, 49–50,
    52–53, 79, 81, 101, 103–105, 107
labor immigration, 98

labor market, 49–50, 53, 95, 98, 103, 110
labor organizations, 112, 138
labor unions, 132, 139, 142
large-scale enterprises, 60, 117–118, 160
liberal economic policies, 68, 146
liberalism, 68–69, 136–137, 139, 141
life expectancy, 15, 92, 157
living conditions, 53, 101, 107
living standards, 14, 53, 157
local government, 143–144

Malthusian crisis, 80
Manchester Liberalism, 68
manorial system, 24
Marx, Karl, 43, 52, 68, 123
mercantilism, 136
migration, 45, 53, 87, 89–90, 94–96, 98–99, 101–102, 154
mixed banking, 64, 113, 115, 117
monetary policy, 23, 71
Munich Coinage Treaty, 35
municipal governments, 143

national product, 13–14, 16–17, 20–22, 44, 144
nationwide railway system, 139
natural population movement, 89
Net National Product, 14, 17, 22, 144
nominal wages, 108
non-tariff restrictions, 84
North German Confederation, 9–11, 37

organized capitalism, 137, 160
overseas migration, 94, 101

pauperism, 14, 141
pension, 110, 142
pig iron, 54–57
political involvement of entrepreneurs, 132

political parties, 132, 142
polytechnical schools, 107
population growth, 47, 50–52, 87–91, 94, 101, 103, 147
protectionism, 86, 137, 145, 151–152
protectionist movements, 152
protective tariffs, 32, 75, 80, 140, 152, 160
Prussian Customs Union, 9, 32, 34
Prussian monetary and financial policy, 71
Prussian reform, 25, 27, 69
Prussian State Bank, 69–70
public health conditions, 91

railway iron, 55–56
railways, 21, 44, 54, 58–68, 113, 117, 139–140, 146, 153
real national product, 13–14
real wages, 13–14, 108–109
Reichsbank, 37, 115
Reichsdeputationshauptschluß, 7n. 3
Rhineland, 125
Rostow's Stages of Economic Growth, 20

Saar region, 19, 70, 137
Saxony, 4, 9, 66, 94, 125, 127
school qualifications, 129
Schumpeter, Joseph, 123
secondary sector, 50, 103
semi-skilled workers, 105
Silesia, 19, 26, 48–49, 66–67, 69–70, 127, 136–137
skilled workers, 105, 107, 112
social insurance, 93, 115, 137, 139, 142
social insurance program, 93, 142
social problems, 138
social question, 141
Sozialistengesetz of 1878, 142
standard of living, 14, 53, 104, 148
state intervention, 59, 110, 136

steam engine, 19, 54, 56–57
steamships, 80, 146
Stein-Hardenberg reforms, 71
strike movements, 112, 138
system of tariffs, 31, 81

tariff law, 141
tariff policy, 81, 83, 138, 140, 152
tariff protection, 83–85
tariff system, 137
tariffs, 9, 31–32, 55, 57, 75, 80–83, 85, 112, 140–141, 152, 160
tertiary sector, 103
textile production, 19, 53
Third Reich, 138, 158
trade liberalization, 146
trade unions, 112, 132
transnational migration, 94
Treaty of Versailles, 158

underemployment, 38, 60, 107
unemployment, 50, 107–108, 111–112, 141, 158
unskilled workers, 51, 105, 112

Upper Silesia, 19, 66–67, 70, 136–137
urban workers, 86, 139

Vienna Coinage Treaty, 36

wage labor, 45, 49–50, 98
wages, 13–14, 45, 53, 79, 101, 107–109, 128, 141, 148, 158
Weimar Republic, 158
welfare capitalism, 139
welfare system, 143
working and living conditions, 53
working class, 52, 110, 141–142
working time, 107–108
World War I, xvi, 11, 89, 103, 108, 112, 118, 141, 154, 157
World War II, 158

Zollverein, 8–10, 23, 31, 33–38, 45, 57, 71
Zollverein coin, 36